If your heart is like my heart,
then give me your hand.

—John Wesley

Sher Stafford

IF YOUR
HEART
IS LIKE
MY
HEART

IF YOUR HEART IS LIKE MY HEART

A Pilgrimage of Faith & Health

SHANE STANFORD & SCOTT MORRIS
WITH SUSAN MARTINS MILLER

LEAFWOOD
PUBLISHERS

an imprint of Abilene Christian University Press

IF YOUR HEART IS LIKE MY HEART

A Pilgrimage of Faith and Health

LEAFWOOD
P U B L I S H E R S
an imprint of Abilene Christian University Press

LIBRARY OF CONGRESS CATALOGING-IN-PUBLICATION DATA
Names: Stanford, Shane, 1970- author.
Title: If your heart is like my heart : a pilgrimage of faith and health /
    Shane Stanford and Scott Morris, with Susan Martins Miller.
Description: Abilene : Leafwood Publishers, 2017.
Identifiers: LCCN 2016040177 | ISBN 9780891124061 (pbk.)
Subjects: LCSH: Church work with the sick—Case studies. | Church Health
    Center—Biography. | Healing—Religious aspects—Christianity. | Medical
    care—Religious aspects—Christianity.
Classification: LCC BV4460 .S73 2017 | DDC 261.8/32109226819—dc23
LC record available at https://lccn.loc.gov/ 2016040177

Published in association with MacGregor Agency, Manzanita, Oregon.

Cover design by ThinkPen Design, LLC
Interior text design by Sandy Armstrong, Strong Design

Leafwood Publishers is an imprint of Abilene Christian University Press
ACU Box 29138
Abilene, Texas 79699

1-877-816-4455
www.leafwoodpublishers.com

17 18 19 20 21 22 / 7 6 5 4 3 2 1

ACKNOWLEDGMENTS

It is only through the patience of those who mean so much to me, both personally and professionally, that this book came to be. As with every project, there are those who stand by me, cheer me on, and say the right things at the right moment so that what God is saying in my heart might land on the page. For each of you—thank you!

However, there are always those who have contributed in very special ways. To Chip MacGregor, your counsel and support continue to set the boundaries for where the path leads. Now, almost ten books later, you are more than an agent; you are a dear and treasured friend.

To everyone at Christ Church, thank you for making a job more than a job and a church feel like home. Your prayers and support are both the foundation and ballast for my calling. I love you more than . . . yes, even words.

To dear friends and colleagues who continue to make this path mean so much, thank you for both your patience and encouragement to say the "next thing."

To Maxie, your guidance and wisdom continue to transform my life and view of God's grace at all the right edges.

To Anita, as I have said so many times before, your assistance, patience, and perseverance always keep the truly important matters ahead of the chronically urgent. This journey would not be possible without you by my side.

To countless family and friends, thank you for your prayers, care, and support by selflessly sharing your heart with me.

To Susan, thank you for crafting an extraordinary message from, too often, what seemed very ordinary words. You are as exceptional a person as you are an author.

To Scott, thank you for making an already busy and extraordinary life accessible and available for me to walk alongside. I could not respect and admire a person more than I do you. Certainly, you are the real deal, my friend, and I am honored if my heart were to resemble yours even in the smallest way.

To my sweet Pokey, Sarai Grace, Juli Anna, and Emma Leigh. Thank you for offering me your hearts when mine seemed too wounded or burdened to go on. I love you all.

And, as always, to my friend, the Nazarene Carpenter, as I have said many times—I stand amazed by what you make beautiful. I stand in awe of how you do it.

—Shane Stanford

The Church Health Center has been around for thirty years, so there are a great many people to thank. I am so grateful for our remarkable staff that has felt the call to do the work we do. The same is true for our board members and volunteers. Fundamentally, it has been a blessing to be a part of the tens of thousands of lives who have come through our doors.

I specifically want to thank the senior leaders of the Church Health Center. Ann Langston, Jenny Bartlett-Prescott, Jennie Robbins, Mike Sturdivant, and Lois McFarland: your leadership has kept our mission alive.

To Rob Carter, Brad Martin, John Stokes, Mason Hawkins, and Bob Buckman, thank you for standing with me.

To Staley Cates, you are like a brother.

To John Kilzer, you are my blood brother.

To Chip and Shane, this doesn't happen without the two of you. Thank you.

To Susan Martins Miller, you are a brilliant writer, editor, and advisor. I feel blessed to work with you.

Most importantly, to my wife, Mary. Every day I am with you, God has smiled on me. You are wise and loving. Thank you for being my partner in this work and in life.

—Scott Morris

A NOTE TO
THE READER

This book is a journey of two friends through the course of years where mostly we did not even know each other, or at least not well. But, in the years after our friendship began and then blossomed, we realized that though we had not known each other personally during the twists and turns of our individual paths, we certainly understood and valued each other's encounters and experiences. That was the first revelation in what became a friendship full of revelations of how God connects people together, although they may appear to be from very different places, generations, or backgrounds. This journey is the unfolding of God's story within the narrative of two people who, for most of it, did not know each other but certainly knew of the hopes and fears that would cause their paths to intersect and mean so much to the other.

However, in sharing the journey, it became necessary to organize the story's "voice" in a single form so that readers might engage the most important part of the picture: the power of God to bring two hearts together around issues that are supposed to change people's lives. Therefore, we wrote in the primary voice of the Rev. Stanford while laying the voice of Dr. Morris faithfully upon the context and conversation of each lesson learned. With the fantastic support of Susan Martins Miller, we just as easily could have flipped the voices or encouraged another editorial form or style. We hope the path we have taken accomplishes the most important objective: that you, the reader, will walk away from our encounter transformed because of our time together.

Thank you for taking the time to hear our story. Blessings and enjoy.

Shane Stanford
Scott Morris
Susan Martins Miller

CONTENTS

1

FEAST FOR FRIENDS

When opportunity knocks, answer.

Darrell was no stranger to church. His mother, Martha, was the unpaid church secretary for the Memphis, Tennessee, congregation where Darrell grew up attending Sunday school. His church home was an important part of his family's life.

But when Darrell acquired AIDS in 1988, no one at church would talk to him.

The pastor told Martha that while he would "be there" for her, he could not do the same for Darrell.

Understandably, that could have been the end of Darrell's connection to a church. Pressing through hurt and disappointment was not easy. But with some encouragement, Darrell found

15

St. John's United Methodist Church, where welcoming members wiped away rejection. Darrell felt so at home that he began to challenge the congregation to a new ministry—a regular meal for people infected with HIV.

Keep in mind this was nearly thirty years ago. Misinformation about how the virus spread inflamed public fear. Even doctors hesitated to have patients with HIV mingle with other patients in casual ways.

But the people at St. John's were most interested in the practical questions. Who would be in charge of the kitchen for such a meal?

"My mama will," Darrell said.

And so Feast for Friends was launched. Twice a month, Martha prepared a main meal and dessert—always three cakes.

By the time I moved to Memphis and learned of Feast for Friends, Darrell had been gone for many years. Just a year after the meal began, Darrell contracted histoplasmosis pneumonia, which led to his death. He was thirty-two.

Martha did not put away her apron. She continued cooking and baking, and every first and third Monday, dozens of people gathered—anyone infected with or affected by HIV.

I moved to Memphis in 2011 to begin my work as senior pastor of Christ United Methodist Church.

And I was HIV-positive.

Dr. Scott Morris, associate pastor at St. John's and founder of the Church Health Center in Memphis, invited my family and me to Feast for Friends.

Martha seemed a little embarrassed that the Feast could only afford to serve hot dogs that night. It wasn't long before I was huddling in conversation with Martha to learn more about their simple needs, and by the time the evening ended, I had promised that my congregation would help.

Confluence of Influence

I contracted HIV in a transfusion to treat the hemophilia I was born with. People with hemophilia experience agonizing pain when joints and muscles bleed internally, and the healing process is slow and requires great care. All through my life, I've wrestled with being careful not to get hurt while also experiencing life to the fullest. My health journey with hemophilia and HIV is part of a greater unfolding of faith and health in my life that raised my awareness of ripening questions in communities I lived among.

As a teenager, I made one new friend in particular, a girl named Pokey. We became inseparable, with hearts open wide for what God planned for us. In May of 1987, I preached my first sermon. I did not know then that I would become a pastor. I only knew I had God's truth on my heart and wanted to share it with others. I chose Philippians 4:6–7 for my text: "Do not worry about anything, but in everything by prayer and supplication with thanksgiving let your requests be made known to God. And the peace of God, which surpasses all understanding, will guard your hearts and minds in Christ Jesus."

In my young lifetime of living with an illness for which there were few treatments and certainly not a cure, I had learned that the body and the spirit heal in the same way. We have to wait with patience, but we can be certain that God comes to us with love and hope even in seasons of heartbreak. This is what I shared in my first sermon.

Meanwhile, Scott Morris was in Memphis doing what he likes to describe as being "too young and dumb to know it couldn't be done." When I was a teenager learning that I had been infected with HIV, Scott Morris had finished seminary, medical school, and a family practice residency. He moved to Memphis to open a faith-based health ministry that would serve the working uninsured in one of the poorest cities in the United States. A few months after my first sermon, in September 1987, Scott saw his first patients at the Church Health Center.

Scott and I did not meet for nearly twenty-five years after my first sermon and his first patient, but the years were not fallow. If I had met Scott in 1987, I might have nodded my head at what he had to say about the confluence of faith and health. After all, I had preached about healing of both body and spirit. But perhaps I would not yet have echoed the bottomless conviction that compelled Scott to challenge people of faith to journey toward wholeness, not merely physical health in a clinical sense.

For a quarter of a century, Scott and I have been on pilgrimages of faith and health. In our own lives, and in our work, every day we meet wayfarers who need encouragement. If not for my medical conditions, Scott and I might have circled each other at Methodist clergy events without knowing each other well. But I was in a new city and needed a new set of doctors for my complex conditions. Dr. Fred Hatch, a nephrologist, was a member of my congregation and a volunteer at the Church Health Center. He said nobody knew more doctors than Scott Morris.

So Pokey—yes, I married my high school sweetheart—and I had lunch with Scott. We talked about my medical needs, of course. Scott did indeed know the best doctors in Memphis. But we also inhaled the redolence of blossoming friendship, and Scott invited us to Feast for Friends.

Not long after that, we went to a football game together at the Liberty Bowl in Memphis. We'd been invited to sit in a box, which Scott had never done in that venue, and we walked around and around the concourse looking for where we were supposed to go. On about the third trip around, my limp was obvious. Scott knew that meant I was bleeding into my ankle. I downplayed what was happening. In my experience, bleeding into my ankle was common.

For that day, I just wanted to watch football with my family and new friends.

Scott was the one who wouldn't let go—a character trait I've come to admire in him. Because of extreme stress in the previous several years, I wasn't taking care of myself the way I should have been. I was weary of managing every little symptom, or even the big ones. I was jaded with going to doctors. Scott saw through all that and realized I needed more than referrals to new specialists. I needed to get a complicated list of problems under control or I was headed for a train wreck. Ultimately, with Scott's help, I went to the Mayo Clinic.

Because Scott became my companion in navigating my medical care, we had frequent opportunities to talk about faith and health in general. The more we talked, the more we saw the ways our journeys intersected.

A portal opened, and I fell through to a new world.

I recognized parts of this faith-health place because I had visited it as a patient. It was no mystery to me how the condition of my body could cloud the condition of my spirit, or how the strength of my spirit could be my greatest weapon in times of physical crisis. I'd also visited this intersection as a pastor, helping people in my congregations, or in the community, draw upon faith to fight physical and emotional disappointments.

Viewing the same landscape from the perspective of a doctor opened my eyes to new colors. I understood the unity of faith and health from a theological perspective—in my case, the Christian gospel. I just wasn't used to seeing such skin-on incarnation of the truth by someone who functioned day-to-day in the medical system.

I knew lots of doctors, even Christian doctors.

But what was going on at the Church Health Center blew my mind.

When Scott Morris came to Memphis to open the Church Health Center, he had no real connections to the city. No building. No money. No staff. No network of old college friends. No job. He was starting from scratch. He came because he read somewhere that it was the poorest city in America. He had to get the medical community—strangers—on board with what he wanted to do. He had to get churches—more strangers—on board. He had to find people—generous strangers—who were willing to reach into their pockets and believe in him.

This was no easy feat for a "too young and dumb" pastor-doctor.

By the time I discovered the Church Health Center, it was a thriving organization bursting at the seams—growing out of fourteen buildings with still never enough space. The clinic that saw twelve patients on its first day now served about seventy thousand patients. A thousand doctors volunteered. A wellness facility saw more than one hundred thousand visits a year for exercise, advice on nutrition, life coaching, support groups, counseling, and more. The Church Health Center was making serious inroads into changing a community and transforming the way people understood their health. Faith was at the core of the Church Health Center—a gathering point, rather than a dividing point.

The questions welled up in me: How can I be part of this? How can my church be part of it?

I encountered the Church Health Center when it was well formed and forward moving. Over time, through the many conversations that followed, the remarkable story unfolded for me more fully.

At the Gate

I see two problems we're trying to overcome when we talk about health care in the larger society. First, we don't view health from an integrated perspective. Health is not just a system of services but the way humans should exist together. Second, we've forgotten that at the heart of being healthy is the truth that no one is on this path alone.

A story my mind often goes to when I ponder faith and health is that of the man with leprosy who came to Jesus. Obviously, he had a severe condition. Now, leprosy is rare and can be treated. Two thousand years ago, it struck fear in whole communities. People with leprosy lived away from family and friends, away from love, away from touch. They might have had to call out "leper" if another person came near or suffer being pelted by rocks to make them put more distance between themselves and others.

How many people did their best every day to avoid even acknowledging the existence of a person with leprosy? How many turned their eyes away and walked past quickly out of fear of becoming infected?

This was the existence of the man every day—until the day Jesus walked by. Perhaps the man took his chances coming close because he knew Jesus's reputation for healing. When he saw Jesus, he said, "If you choose, you can make me clean."

And Jesus was willing. "I do choose," he said. He didn't avert his eyes and hurry past. He heard the man's voice. He stopped. He touched. He healed.

For me that is a helpful pattern to use to think about faith and health, especially as I absorb the work of the Church Health Center. I have felt like that man at times—with diseases people are afraid of, including doctors. As a pastor, I knew Jesus would want his followers to act with healing compassion, but as Darrell learned, that doesn't always happen, even in churches. People feel ostracized and worn out. They feel ignored, unseen, alone. They can sit on the sidelines of their own communities and watch the people walking right past them with no thought of helping them. I'm sure I have done this many times when I was weighted with my own worries.

But Jesus stopped. He *saw* the man and he *chose* to respond.

The Church Health Center sees people and chooses to respond. That's why I've been so enthusiastic to have my congregation involved in their work.

Anthropologist Margaret Mead said, "Never doubt that a small group of thoughtful, committed people can change the world. Indeed, it's the only thing that ever has." I think she's right.

A little girl comes to the doctor with a stomachache because her daddy left the family.

A teenager injures his shoulder doing construction work to support the family because his mother has breast cancer.

After forty days of no improvement, it's time for a husband to take his comatose wife off the ventilator.

A young woman who just lost a leg gets to the specialists and counselors who can help her believe in the future again.

Scott Morris is a doctor, but he never forgets that he is a pastor. He has more to give his patients than pills and clinical information. As a senior pastor, I have more to give than Sunday sermons and budget-committee meetings. This journey of faith and health is about discovering lessons that gleam in the ordinary. It's about polishing hope until it reflects light. It's about illuminating our kindred longings.

We meet people every day with questions about their lives looming over their heads. So many patients, church members, friends, and staff in our own circles have known heartache with the potential to cripple their lives. For some it does, and they stare into a spiritual abscess without the consolation of hope for change. Others—even in similar circumstances—somehow see light and meaning and inspire us to imagine a future vast with hope and healing.

Life, or at least a particular season of life, may seem like one enormous question mark. We don't claim to have all the answers, but we believe responses that bring health to both body and spirit begin with willingness to ask the questions.

That is what this book is about. Scott always has a story with more punch than any lecture. We will tell stories from our own lives, and we will introduce people we've met on the journey to faith and health.

And if you're asking, "But what can I *do*?" we're going to help with that as well.

Together we will discover that we don't have to lie awake at night pondering life's great questions and letting them fester. Instead we can step into life with confidence, joy, and anticipation.

COMMUNITY CARES

When I fell through the portal that the Church Health Center opened, my sight changed. It was like getting new lenses in my glasses that brought into focus what before had been blurry around the edges.

Congregations sometimes need to get new glasses. The old lenses look at their communities and see heritage. People remember what used to be. We hear it in their language and see the wistful look in their eyes. But the life cycles of faith communities eventually take them to times of transition. An event may thrust the congregation into a new season, or members may open their eyes and realize the old ways will not take them toward the future. Transition becomes a time either to see themselves and the larger community through lenses of their potential or to become sedentary in a transition that signals the end. Congregations either will get moving and do something or passively surrender to the inevitable.

Let me suggest five places congregations ought to look if they choose to embrace transition by setting themselves in motion in their own communities.

1. What are the larger community's prevailing worship styles and trends? Are most of the congregations primarily traditional or primarily leaning toward contemporary expression of faith? Are there congregations with strong ethnic identities?

2. How well do community members care for one another? Where are the places, such as parks and festivals, that the community connects? Or do people tend to stay within their own homes and comfortable neighborhood boundaries?

3. Is this a generous community? When need arises—and it always does—do people respond in generous ways, or do they stand off and hold their resources close?

4. Is the community trying to become better, to be something more—in terms of the arts, shared experiences, and how they engage in dialogue around community concerns?

5. Is it a community that serves? Are people engaging in being the hands and feet of constructiveness together?

When we read in the Bible about the first-century church, it seems to me that these five lenses brought their experience into focus. Looking around, noticing each other, and engaging with each other reveal the potential and possibility of a new and strong community. We don't have to just do the same old thing. We can do the things that no one else is doing to accomplish the things that no one else is accomplishing. Opportunity knocks all around us.

> *God of us all, like the calm of the early morning, may we see with clarity what it takes to follow you. Give us the soul force to march only toward you. Amen.*

2

FAITH AND HEALTH

Abundant life comes from the heart of God.

Here's a story from Scott that introduces an important figure in his experience of Memphis:

After I'd been in Memphis for a while, I heard about William Austin, a sharecropper in Tipton County, Tennessee, during the 1940s and 1950s. He had seventeen children, because to be a successful farmer you needed your own workforce.

In the early 1960s, two of William's sons left the life of sharecropping for jobs in Memphis. Eventually they persuaded William to follow them, and he became a sanitation worker for the City of Memphis. As time went on, William's children gave him grandchildren. On Sunday afternoons, William would gather his grandchildren and talk about life. He focused a lot on how to treat people, emphasizing that people are all the same—even white people. William hadn't always believed that, but during the famous 1968 strike of the sanitation workers, during which Martin Luther King Jr. was assassinated, he had come to know of one good white man.

The sanitation workers referred to this one good white man as their secret weapon.

By February 1968, when the strike highlighting the injustice of low wages and poor working conditions seemed intractable, Frank McRae was the youngest district superintendent in the United Methodist Church and well on his way to becoming a bishop if he wanted to be one. But Frank, who grew up in Memphis, was deeply involved in the community outside the church as well.

Mayor Loeb was one of Frank's best friends. When it was evident the strike wouldn't easily be resolved, the mayor needed someone he could trust to be a courier between the mayor's office and the strikers. In his personal views, Frank was clearly on the side of the sanitation workers, but he faithfully shuttled between the two camps as an instrument of reconciliation. On April 5, 1968, the day after Dr. King was shot, the one good white man organized the black and white clergy of Memphis to march behind a cross to the mayor's office and demand an end to the strike.

In the volatile weeks of summer swelter after King was assassinated, the chasm of mistrust and suspicion between the races in Memphis widened. Frank was at the center of an interracial group of ministers who came together to find healing for their city, and the Metropolitan Inter-Faith Association was born. Frank became a powerful influence in dealing with local racial issues.

Years after the sanitation workers' strike, one of William Austin's grandsons, James, came to study and then work in Memphis, where he encountered Frank McRae. As James learned more about Frank, his passion for justice and equality, and his role as a white Methodist minister in the civil rights movement, it dawned on him that Frank was the one good white man his grandfather had told him about.

Grandfather and grandson met Frank decades apart and both saw in him a life committed to justice and equality.

After some time, Frank became senior pastor of St. John's United Methodist Church and led the congregation into an era of being a servant church that consistently responded to emerging needs in the community. Like Martin Luther King Jr., Frank McRae's life was about more than marching. He believed the church exists to make the life of the poor better, including working against the unjust social systems that perpetuate poverty. The Old Testament prophet Amos reminds us of God's priority: "Let justice roll down like waters, and righteousness like an ever-flowing stream" (Amos 5:24). Water seeps into every available crevice. That's how pervasive justice should be.

These convictions made Frank McRae the best person for me to connect with when I arrived in Memphis. And if Frank was a picture of God's justice for the poor, then I wanted to be just like Frank. •

When Scott was about ten years old, a Methodist bishop put his hand on Scott's head and said that someday he would make a good pastor. Scott was more interested in pitching for the Atlanta Braves.

By the time Scott was a teenager, it was beginning to look like the Braves might not call, but the thought of writing sermons every week was enough to give him heart palpitations. If he was going to have a calling in the church, it would look different from most pastoral positions. Reading the Bible, Scott could see that its pages were thick with themes of healing and care for both body and spirit.

Yet what was the church doing?

He heard his congregation praying for people on Sunday morning. The pastor visited people in the hospital. A few other people called on the shut-ins.

Was that all? Couldn't the church do better? Where was the abundant life?

How Did We Get Here?

If you're a patient as much as I am, gratitude for caring doctors is an attitude worth cultivating. I've always been motivated to maintain my insurance status. It's not unusual for young adults to start out in jobs that don't offer employer-provided insurance plans or, because they are young and healthy, to decide to play the odds that they won't get sick until they can get themselves financially established and can afford the premiums. Even under the Affordable Care Act, people will choose to have penalties withheld from income tax refunds rather than pay more expensive premiums.

Between hemophilia and HIV, I didn't have that option. My early decisions about marriage and employment revolved around their impact on my insured status, so I've never had trouble understanding the anxiety that comes from the threat of losing insurance, the resignation of not being able to afford it, or the obstacles to care that result from the lack of it.

I do sometimes wonder how we got ourselves in this situation where caring for the sick has become one of those topics we cannot raise at the dinner table because of the risk that we won't be able to speak to each other about it with civility.

Scott is not afraid of the topic, and he gives a cogent explanation dozens of times of year when he speaks on the topic, especially to the faith community.

The Bible is full of miraculous healings, but the earliest Christians also expected healing would come through the practice of medicine. The best information doctors of the time had at their disposal was largely guesswork from our twenty-first-century viewpoint, but at the time people had faith that God was able and willing to heal through these methods just as we have faith that God is able and willing to heal through the methods available to us now.

By the fourth century, the Christian faith had spread around the Roman Empire. Tradition suggests that Helena, mother of the emperor Constantine, was the first to open a hospital. The ancient world had no system to care for the sick—especially sick who were also poor—until Christians offered hospitals. Julian, a fourth-century Roman emperor, did not have much use for Christians, which earned him the moniker "Julian the Apostate." Yet even Julian could not deny what happened when Christians cared for the poor. "Now we can see," he wrote, "what it is that makes those Christians such powerful enemies of our gods. It is the brotherly love which they manifest toward the sick and poor, the thoughtful manner in which they care for the dead, and the purity of their own lives."

During the Middle Ages, when intellectual pursuits and culture stagnated, people who got sick went to see the monks. The Crusades introduced hospitals along the travel routes. Christians kept medical learning and practice alive.

As every school student learns in a basic world-history class, by the eighteenth and nineteenth centuries, scientific knowledge exploded. Unfortunately, the church did not do very well at keeping up. Eventually medicine became a rival to religion, which seemed to be less and less necessary for understanding how the human body works. Caring for the body separated from caring for the spirit. Spirituality, it was thought, had no place in understanding what happened in the body.

Despite this rift, the church still had a role. Someone had to provide a place where scientific advances took practical form, and that was once again people of faith.

In Massachusetts, Cotton Mather was as zealous about physical health as he was about preaching on spiritual matters. A pastor in Boston, he was also a significant figure in Colonial medicine and instrumental in developing an inoculation for smallpox. In England, John Wesley believed keeping people healthy was essential to ministry. He advocated fresh air, clean water, and daily exercise, and he opened dispensaries to serve the poor.

In the early twentieth century, Christian denominations began opening hospitals in increasing numbers. The well-to-do continued to call physicians into their homes to care for them, but the poor went to hospitals. Eventually, though, even the wealthy had to admit that people in hospitals had better results, and hospitals began to open up to everyone. Churches, however, had trouble keeping up with paying for all this, especially as technology became more expensive.

Then in 1965, the legislation that created Medicare and Medicaid poured federal money into funding hospitals. Now medicine began to be an industry unto itself. No longer did it make sense for religious organizations to own hospitals, especially flailing ones, and a lot of hospitals went on the market. Half a century later we might still see denominational words in hospital names, but for the most part the churches no longer own the facilities. Profitability often eclipsed a vision to care for the poor.

What happened in the space of a century? Hospitals evolved from caring for the poor without charge to seeking profitability.

Once again body and spirit were separated.

Once again the health care system neglected the poor.

And the national conversation about our obligation to care for the sick has taken yet another form.

When Scott speaks on this subject, he seems certain that in the past the church did a better job of being a healing presence in society than it has done in the last fifty or sixty years. My first sermon as a teenager was about faith and healing, and so was Scott's. A leader in his church youth group, he was always at the ready to preach on the annual Youth Sunday. His topic was consistent from year to year—that faith and health should not exist in two separate spheres but be united.

After high school he went to the University of Virginia for no better reason than that an English teacher thought he would like it. His choice of a seminary was more strategic. "Eventually I would have to figure out how to go to medical school," he says, "but for now I needed a seminary that did not think I was off my rocker for wanting to combine medicine and ministry." Scott wrote to Emory, Duke, Yale, Harvard, and a handful of other schools to inquire if he could combine medicine and religion in his studies. The responses generally were along two lines: either it was a nutty idea, or the notion was intriguing but the school did not offer a program that would accommodate him.

Yale, on the other hand, mailed back a ten-page statement on how Scott could do what he wanted to do. Surprisingly, he discovered, few divinity school students at Yale planned on being parish pastors. Up until that point, he had been battered by plenty of opinions that what he wanted to do couldn't—or shouldn't—be done. But at Yale, everybody seemed to have an outrageous idea. In that way he was in a like-minded setting for the first time in his life.

Scott gravitated to the chaplain of Yale's medical school, who also taught in the divinity school. One day Scott was in the chaplain's small office waiting to talk to him. A lot of Yale's historic buildings were showing their age, the kind of places where the stony mustiness of centuries permeates. In one of these venerable buildings, the chaplain's office was not much more than a crowded cubicle. On a corner of his desk was a stack of brochures, one of them titled *How to Start a Church-Based Health Clinic* by Granger Westberg.

Scott's heart thudded against his ribs. Words and phrases jumped out at him. The pamphlet was only twenty pages long, yet its basic idea of a church-based health clinic captured Scott's imagination and has never left him.

This was *exactly* what he wanted to do, and now he discovered that others were trying to do it as well. Westberg was a Lutheran pastor and hospital chaplain who opened a health clinic in a United Church of Christ basement in Hinsdale, Illinois, outside Chicago. It was the first of a string of locations that Westberg called wholistic health centers.

The next day Scott was on the phone to Granger Westberg, asking a thousand questions. That summer he went to Chicago to see the way the clinic worked. Later, during medical school, he spent a month at the clinic in Hinsdale, Illinois, learning all he could about Granger's views of *whole person* health care. At last he had a concrete idea about how to begin binding body and spirit. This quest eventually took Scott to Memphis in 1986, but not before he had a chance to try out the idea for himself.

Here's Scott:

• • • • • • • • During my medical residency, when my plans for a church-based health clinic were becoming well formed, I met Dr. Cullen Rivers, a pulmonologist. When he heard about my aims, he told me of an area known as Crossover where he was involved, as well as a storefront church in downtown Richmond.

"Do you think we could start something there?" he said.

"I'd love to give it a try." It was intriguing to me to develop a prototype while I was still a resident.

The next Saturday, Cullen and I visited the church. The front of the building had chairs set up in rows and an old pulpit. In the back room, we pondered whether we could use the space for a clinic.

Cullen was doubtful. "This is pretty rough."

But I could see possibilities. "Let's try. We can hang sheets and create a couple of rooms. What do we have to lose?"

The next week, we held our first clinic, and five people from the church showed up to see the doctor. Over the next two years, we recruited a half dozen physicians to help us on Saturdays, and I became chair of a loosely bound group of agencies, split between secular and religious organizations. Richmond Street Center came into being to form a single point of service for the homeless. The third floor of a renovated building would house a medical clinic. A year later they received a federal grant to hire a full-time physician. · · · · · · · ·

Social Conscience or Do-Gooder?

These days Scott doubts anyone remembers he was ever in Richmond, but starting that part-time clinic was his personal testing ground for what he would eventually attempt in Memphis on a much larger scale with the intention of being in it for the long haul.

The health-care crisis in the United States, even in the 1980s, was rampant enough that free clinics and government-subsidized clinics had their place in caring for specific parts of the population or addressing particular conditions, but neither model was what Scott had in mind. Rather, the vision was to create a primary-care practice that was a medical home—a place where the working uninsured could come for the care that would help keep them healthy, not a place that focused on crisis situations or specific diseases. Patients of the Church Health Center would know they had a doctor they could count on, a name to write on a form that asked who their doctor is. The ministry also would reach people in churches and help them have healthier, more fulfilling lives.

We all have moments when we ponder why we do what we do—and how well we do it. Here's Scott:

· · · · · · · · I once received an odd note from a doctor. We had sent him a letter thanking him for volunteering to treat a patient for us during the previous year. He responded to our thanks by saying he did not deserve it and added a postscript: "Don't you get tired of being a do-gooder?"

Most of us spend our childhoods avoiding the label of *do-gooder*. Somehow it suggests we are not interesting or fully rounded people. To me it sounded like someone who is deadly dull, which of course I don't want to be.

On the other hand, while being a do-gooder is why I became involved in care for the poor, the truth is I do get tired. I have no doubt that there are times when others perceive me as doing good and my mind is off to a distant place. These types of experiences help me understand that it is not just doing good that I strive for, but doing good with a pure heart. The doctor's comment unsettled me not because he touched a nerve going back to my childhood, but because I knew so clearly that his perception of me was not right. When I was younger and played sports, I was sometimes good enough to win without doing my best, and I was content with the outcome. Even in the work I do now, I find myself sometimes being willing to settle for a good effort rather than giving my best.

I must change a great deal in my thoughts and actions before I can accept the title of do-gooder. In conversations within the church or in the wider society, the same issue threatens us. The lure to do only an adequate job when it comes to health care is strong. But that's not good enough. I am convinced that God means for us to do our best at every turn. ·

Scott was not just a doctor with a social conscience—though he is that. He was a United Methodist minister committing his professional future to caring for the poor. If he was going to open a church-based health clinic—and he was determined to—it would be because the clinic was fundamentally about the church.

Embodying the love of God as Jesus did.

Offering a message of hope to the community.

Caring for the least among us with the love of God.

Living out the truth that abundant life comes from the heart of God.

Scott got a job with the public health department in Memphis to support himself and began the process of ferreting out who would want to join this impossible venture. One of his first communications, even before moving to Memphis, was with the senior pastor of St. John's United Methodist Church in Memphis—Frank McRae, the "one good white man" of the 1968 sanitation workers strike. Prevailing on their common credentials as Methodist clergy, Scott introduced himself in a letter, laid out the vision, and dared to suggest that Frank's church ought to be the first partner.

"I hope you are not scared off by this mass of paper I have sent you," Scott wrote.

· · · · · · · · · ·   I thought, however, it would be helpful for you to get to know some of my ideas and where I come from before we meet . . . I am interested in a health clinic which is part of a church's ministry, but with wide ecumenical support. . . . The targeted population would be the working poor.

The reasons for beginning such a health care program in the church, to my way of thinking, are straightforward. First and foremost, the biblical and historical witness of the church demands that we care for the sick. In many ways, we have abdicated this role during the twentieth century . . . Secondly, the medical profession is not very well suited to care for many of the problems that people bring to physicians. Problems of aging, stress, chronic disease, and preventive medicine do not need the extreme specialization that most physicians today have. These are issues of ongoing *care,* and yet medicine is built around ways to obtain *cure.* The church, however, not physicians, functions best in matters that call for ongoing care. •

Once Scott moved to Memphis, Frank introduced him to three doctors in the St. John's congregation. One, an older internist, teetered on the height of suspicion about what this new young doctor wanted to do. No matter how many times Scott explained his idea for a church-based health ministry, his fellow physician could not see the link between being a pastor and being a doctor. Like so many people, he saw the two vocations as nonoverlapping spheres and suspected Scott planned to spend his time praying for people rather than practicing quality primary care.

Because he couldn't get his head around the premise of uniting faith and health, the doctor fought the idea of the Church Health Center at every turn within St. John's. Fortunately, most of the congregation was open to supporting the new ministry. Even after the Church Health Center opened and Scott was on the pastoral staff of the church, the internist came to church every week armed with an article he had torn from the most recent *New England Journal of Medicine* or some other professional publication he was convinced wasn't already in Scott's reading pile.

This went on for *ten years.*

Why should churches be concerned about health care? Because Jesus was. Healing is as much a part of the Christian message today as it was in the first century or the fourth century. The body is sacred. People of faith—not just Christians—can reclaim the body, life, and death, and then rethink models for prevention, care, and conversation. And while the topic is worthy of public discourse and even legislation, there's no reason people of faith must sit back and wait to see what the government is going to do. We can begin at our own dinner tables.

Jewish and Christian sacred texts share stories of the presence of God among the people. To this day, Orthodox Jews believe that the Shekinah, the glory of God come to dwell among humans, never left the temple mount even after the temple was destroyed in AD 70 and not rebuilt. They pray at the Western Wall, all that remains of the temple, because they believe God is still there. It is still holy ground, and not just to the Jews but to Muslims and Christians as well.

I like the question Scott asks about this: "What makes a place holy or an event sacred?" And even better, I like his answer: "It's the movement of God in what transpires. Are we on holy ground? This is the question for living faithful lives of love and joy that take people closer to God. We know we stand on holy ground when we seek God there, live out our faith there, respond to our calling there, and expect and welcome God's presence."

Where is holy ground when it comes to questions of health and health care? Where will we see the movement of God in what transpires?

Into the Dark

Before I moved to Memphis, I lived for two and a half years in Florida. I was sent to be the senior pastor of a church of 4,500 outside Pensacola. On the surface the church looked like a progressive congregation, but I soon learned its history involved one struggle after another.

I became the latest struggle.

A faction of the church was antagonistic toward me because they believed that every person who was HIV-positive had done something to deserve being sick, such as abusing drugs or being gay. I was no exception to their outlandish conclusions. I was HIV-positive, so therefore I was guilty of some dark disorder.

On the Saturday before my first sermon—before these people even knew me—someone slashed all the tires of my car. Just to be sure, they also slashed the tires of my mother-in-law's car and my parents' car. All our vehicles had Mississippi license plates, so we were easy to identify. A few days later, someone urinated on the sofa in my office, destroyed my computer, and defecated on the walls. I started getting hate mail.

This was the church's response to illness?

Two things occurred to me at the time. First, people believed they were standing up for what they were sure was right. The problem was that they were doing it with hate and no effort at all to understand the situation from someone else's point of view. Conversation, much less compassion, about my complex medical situation was never on their minds. This challenged me to think about how I frame situations and conversations in my own life.

Do I jump to conclusions? Do I make up my mind without being open to the possibility that another perspective exists and may hold truth?

And if those people came to me now to ask forgiveness, would I be able to offer it?

Second, I thought about a doctor who cared for me for many years, carefully and compassionately sorting out my medical issues but also seeing me as a person in every encounter I had with her. Dr. Nancy taught me that you love someone regardless of the way the person behaves.

So I stayed in Florida for two and a half years. And it was hell.

I would preach my heart out and hear nothing to tell me that my words were sinking in. The stress of those years is the primary reason I arrived in Memphis so fatigued from trying to take care of myself that a crisis was imminent.

Now, years later, I receive letters that say, "You don't know me, but I was in church, and the words you spoke changed my life. They made me read the Bible and treat my neighbor better."

The abundant life comes from the heart of God.

COMMUNITY CARES

The impact of what we do may not be realized immediately or be in the form that we hope for. When it comes to health care, I have more opportunities than most people to contend with this question. But my medical needs should not set me apart from other people of faith. The question remains whether we are doing what God calls us to do and whether we are doing it with love.

Our blood contains factors that work together to provide two essential functions in the event of an injury. First, the factors, which are switched on in a particular order, cause the blood to coagulate, or clot. Then they help the wound to heal. If you are missing even just one factor, the clotting and healing process is disrupted. People with hemophilia are missing a factor and need to replace it by receiving healthy blood product so that the blood can clot and the body can heal as it was created to do.

Replacing Factor VIII all my life has helped me understand that faith is a replacement factor essential to healing the wounds in our lives and communities. It fills in the gap where we are missing something that we cannot generate on our own. As we do life together, faith makes us accountable to one another. It makes us want to be accessible to one another. Whether the challenge is big or small, faith helps us fit better into how we respond to each other's needs.

Just as replacing the missing factor in the blood allows the body to do what it was created to do, faith allows us to do exactly what we were created to do. Often, people drift toward thinking that in order to accomplish anything significant, we have to very nearly perform miracles. I don't think that's true. Our faith, a gift from God, helps us fill in the blanks of what the world is missing. Missing values. Missing commitments. Missing relationships. Most of all, missing love. In faith, the most common tasks God created and gifted us to do become miraculous because we do them with love. The intrinsic nature of faith is that it replaces what we're missing and allows us to participate in healing work in our families and communities. We don't have to be great theologians or the next Mother Teresa. We only need to recognize our need for faith and to allow faith to do its work in and through us. Then we will share in the abundant life that comes from God's heart.

> *Our God, we are so consumed with the mundane that we rarely see that we are part of a whole that is transcendent. When we are blinded by your unknowable majesty, help us to live each day to the best we are able and follow you on the way. Amen.*

THREE

THROUGH A GLASS DARKLY

*Our job is to make the person
next to us look good.*

Here's Scott:

Mohammed complained of pain down his left leg for over a month. He and his wife owned a convenience store in a rough part of Memphis, and they worked long hours. Although he was in pain and without health insurance, Mohammed was reluctant to seek care from the Church Health Center because he was Muslim and from Pakistan. He was forty-eight years old and had been in Memphis for nine years without health insurance, and still worried about the Christian response to his religion and country.

I did my best to assure Mohammed that the Church Health Center was not a place that would judge his beliefs. The New Testament writer Paul said that we see through a glass darkly, or as more modern translations would say, we see in a mirror, dimly.

We don't know everything. We don't see everything in crisp focus. But we can agree with St. Paul that love makes the difference. When we look at circumstances through the lens of love, we might not be as quick to say who is right and who is wrong. · · · · · · · · · · · · · · ·

There is a truth that is greater than any one individual. Truth can come into being in the community of what people are willing to do together. When enough people dare in the same direction, we achieve momentum and begin to accomplish something. We don't know what we might create together, but we do know that if we let competitive issues distract us from that higher truth, people like Mohammed will suffer.

Everyone's life has brokenness, and everyone has a responsibility to seek wholeness. When you're not well, it affects the entire system in which you live and work and play. I can see this truth in the faces of my wife and daughters when they wonder if I'm doing what I should be doing to take care of myself. In a sense, my brokenness is recorded in the volumes that constitute my medical records. But I, like everyone else, have also known brokenness of spirit, brokenness of relationship, brokenness of trust, brokenness of community.

It's part of our shared humanity that these things are true, and we are more able to move toward wellness and wholeness if we recognize this rather than make every shared problem someone else's responsibility. Our society faces huge challenges when it comes to full, meaningful lives. We want individuals to be well, but we also have a responsibility to seek wholeness for our communities, for our society. We do that by coming together. Pride about who is at the top of the heap doesn't bring constructive change, but it's surprising what humility will do.

Mohammed, with the pain in his leg, is not the only person who dreads being judged and puts off getting care. Can we agree, for instance, that every woman who is pregnant deserves quality care regardless of the circumstances under which she became pregnant? What might happen if a community rallied around prenatal care for the sake of those mothers and babies rather than disputing whether an unmarried, low-income woman with two other small children had any business becoming pregnant?

One of the principles that Scott inculcates at the Church Health Center is that it is our responsibility to make the person next to us look good. In other words, we're all in this together, even in the uncertain parts—which is most of the time, if we're honest. The brokenness in our lives may manifest in different ways, but we lose, rather than gain, when we choose to let the forms of our brokenness put us in competing camps.

Can we make our own worlds big enough to include people who are not like us—and have more impact than we dreamed possible?

Invitation to God's Work

Frank McRae didn't throw Scott's audacious letter in the trash. That was encouraging. Even better, he agreed to meet when Scott came to Memphis.

Frank's job at St. John's United Methodist Church was far from cushy. The church had once been the most prominent Protestant congregation in Memphis and had been known as "the doctors' church" because so many doctors were members. It was a conservative, highbrow church, but its location in midtown, on the edge of downtown, meant it was devastated by the white flight of the 1960s, especially after the assassination of Martin Luther King Jr. not very far away. St. John's was a dying church when Frank took the pulpit. Any pastor accepting this appointment had to know it would be an uphill battle to see the church thrive.

Frank didn't pull any punches. Early on he preached a sermon he called "The Queen Is Dead." If St. John's was going to survive, he said, the congregation had to give up being the queen church and become a servant church. The congregation had to be something more than a gathering place for the old guard pining for historic prestige. It had to be Jesus's hands in the world. Under Frank's leadership, the church launched a rash of new ministries it would not have dabbled in during the old days—a food pantry, outreach to people reluctant to come through the doors, children's ministry. This effort stemmed the bleeding and attracted a wave of younger members.

Frank arranged a meeting between Scott and the old guard of the church at the home of Luther and Lucy Underhill, who lived well east of the deteriorating downtown part of Memphis. This was going to be a tough crowd. They were the people who loved the church when it was *the* church to attend, and mourned—but stayed—when the life cycle of the church was in a downward spiral. They paid the bills and kept the building operating and the pastor's salary up-to-date during times of great hand-wringing about the future.

But they were also the people who sat somewhere else when new young couples like Ann and Dudley Langston unwittingly slid into members' usual pews, who piled up canned goods for the food pantry, who decided that the sound of children in the church halls was not such a bad thing. Ann was an attorney, and Frank had asked her to check out Scott. Her report must have been favorable, because there they were, facing some of the most influential people in the church.

A screeching cackle greeted Scott when he entered the Underhill house. After a startled moment, Scott breathed a sigh of relief. It was a giant parrot chattering, not a hostile hostess. That bird talked nonstop for the entire meeting. Scott did his best to ignore it and focus on presenting a vision for a church-based health clinic. The people gathered in that home could make or break St. John's support for the nascent Church Health Center. Scott hoped they were listening more to him than to the parrot. After the meeting came the stereotypical covered-dish church supper.

"This one seemed to have a theme," Scott remembers. "Instead of baked casseroles, it was fifty varieties of Jell-O salad. That's all there was for dinner—everything you could put in Jell-O. I kid you not."

But even an old-fashioned church potluck can be a sign that a congregation is open to hearing a newfangled invitation to do God's work.

Luke, who wrote one of the four accounts in the Bible of Jesus's life, gives us an interesting glimpse into how Jesus saw his work. Jesus had long full days of preaching, teaching, and healing, and the crowds followed him so closely that his own family couldn't get near. Someone told him, "Your mother and brothers are standing outside."

"Bring them right in," we might expect Jesus to say. "Don't keep them waiting."

Jesus, though, used the incident as a teachable moment. He said, "My mother and my brothers are those who hear the word of God and do it" (Luke 8:20–21). I don't think Jesus was disparaging his earthly family, and quite conceivably they sat down and had a nice meal together at the end of the day. But Jesus's response to the news of his waiting relatives was to invite *all* who had been listening to his parables and sermons, and watching his healing miracles, to participate in God's work.

When I hear stories about the early days of the Church Health Center, that's what I see—an invitation for everyone to participate in doing God's work in the world. That's what Scott was after, and that's the opportunity Frank McRae saw. Scott's purpose was never to persuade anyone to believe everything he believed, but to link arms to discover a greater understanding of what God expects of us.

Frank was working with Scott on finding a building for the Church Health Center. One day they stepped into a house right across the street from St. John's United Methodist Church.

Scott tells the story:

"It was really a fine old house in its day." The real estate agent was almost a caricature. "If you look closely, you can see all the woodworking detail. They just don't build houses like this anymore."

It was all I could do to keep from laughing. Frank and I, with the architect, were looking at a falling-down boardinghouse that had not been cleaned up in years. Every room was subdivided into two padlocked apartments, each barely big enough to hold a bed. Two old tires and a television with a broken picture tube adorned the living room. Underneath the stairway was an oddly placed bathtub with a shower spigot that never stopped dripping.

Most people would have laughed if they knew I was thinking, *This is the perfect place.* I could see in this falling-down house everything I needed in a location to make my lifelong dream of creating a church-based health clinic for the working poor come alive.

As we walked up the stairs, the agent told us the house's history. It had once been the home of Wassell Randolph, a prominent Memphis lawyer and member of the library board, for whom the University of Tennessee's student center is named. As he got older, Randolph was unable to climb the stairs and lived only on the first floor. The awkwardly placed bathtub had been installed for him during his last years.

On Randolph's death, the house was divided into increasingly smaller rooms. At one point, twenty elderly people lived in what was built as four-bedroom home. The police eventually closed it down as a boardinghouse when a family member complained about the poor living conditions. Next it was a brothel. Directly across the street from the church that was once Memphis's most prominent Protestant house of worship, this was an odd place for a brothel, but times change. The church membership had shrunk as the wealthy moved out toward the east. Even the business for ladies of the night was not that good, so they too moved on.

The day we visited the house, a group of young actors from a local theater troupe lived in it. As we walked from one room to the next, I tried to envision the original architecture. Hints of its former beauty were everywhere: the twelve-foot ceilings, the hand-carved moldings, and the hardwood floors.

Now, rotting drywall and flaking paint marred its former glory. After the tour, as the group stood in the yard trashed with odds and ends, the agent asked, "Well, what did you think?"

Frank and architect looked at me.

Without hesitation, I said, "We'll take it." ·

Every time I visit Scott in his office, I climb the stairs over that strange bathroom.

The Church Health Center opened the same fall that I learned the truth about my HIV status. It began with one doctor—Scott—a nurse, and a skeletal administrative staff.

"I wasn't sure anyone would come," Scott says. "My nurse and receptionist were still busy organizing their spaces as I paced nervously through the empty exam rooms. Finally the nurse shooed me upstairs to my office with the assurance that she would call me if we actually got any patients. I still remember listening from upstairs and hearing the front door open.

"Then came that blessed sound: 'May I help you?'

"A mother and daughter had arrived. Fifteen minutes later, after gathering some basic intake information, the nurse called me down.

I don't remember what the little girl's complaint was. It was nothing serious, but it started a course that defined my life. The TV cameras were there, and the next morning the front page of the newspaper featured a photo of my nurse weighing a small child. By the end of the day we had seen twelve patients."

After that day, the Church Health Center never lacked patients. Word of mouth is powerful advertising! A growing reputation for compassionate, high-quality care for people like Mohammed has brought more patients to the Church Health Center than they can see, even though they are now a medical home to seventy thousand people. The waiting list is long, which propels Scott and other leaders to constantly ask how they can help more people and help them better. That question never seems to fade.

Scott went to Memphis because of the number of people in that city for whom routine health care was out of reach. These people often ignored signs of illness because they dreaded the cost of medical care. Then, when a medical condition that could have been easily managed became urgent, they went to the emergency room to see doctors who did not know them and who were not likely to see them again.

During the first year of seeing patients, Scott admitted patients to the hospitals himself. Most of them went to "The Med," a regional publicly funded hospital, but some also went to the Methodist hospital or one of the Catholic facilities. This added to Scott's frenetic running around, obviously, as he tried to care for patients in several hospitals as well as keep clinic hours and meet with people who could potentially support the ongoing operating budget. Once more doctors were saying yes to volunteering service with some predictability, including seeing patients in the hospitals, it was harder for the hospitals to say no to donating their services as well. The Church Health Center became a leveraging point for making better use of resources already present in the system to serve the underserved more efficiently.

Bodily Uncertainty

Pokey is the reason I'm a Methodist—or at least the route I took into the United Methodist Church. After I shared my HIV diagnosis with her, she and I grew closer than ever. My doctor had guessed I might live another three or four years. Whatever time I had left, we wanted to spend it together.

I refused to live under the weight of expecting to get sick. And what at first sounded like a death sentence turned out to be no more than a best guess proven wrong.

I grew up a Southern Baptist, but as a teenager I began attending the small United Methodist Church where Pokey worshipped with her family, and I hit it off with the pastor of her church. In college I studied prelaw, but Reverend Walley, her pastor, saw a different future for me, and I began a part-time job as his assistant. Pokey and I were more than best friends when I learned I was HIV-positive. Young as we were, Pokey and I had talked about getting married for years, almost from the first day we met. Neither of us doubted that God had joined our journeys and we would walk forward together. College and jobs kept us busy, and my health condition complicated the question. But I knew I wanted Pokey at my side, no matter what, and I knew she wanted to be there, no matter what.

We were still in college when I proposed and Pokey accepted. Our friends and family were ecstatic on our behalf. Pokey's parents knew about my HIV status, but they also knew that Pokey and I were approaching the challenges ahead of us with our eyes wide open. Most couples as young as we were—and with a lot of education still ahead of us—would have planned to wait several years to get married. The people closest to us knew that our circumstances meant we might not have several years. However, if I married while I was in college, I would lose my health insurance, and with both hemophilia and HIV, that was no small consideration. Most twenty-year-olds have little health history of concern to insurance companies eager to sell them a policy, but in my case it was not an option to try to buy health insurance independently. Being without insurance was a frightening picture. We both needed good jobs and health benefits before we could set a date for our wedding. As anxious as we were to be husband and wife, we had to be patient for God's provision.

While I still had no symptoms of HIV, blood work showed that my immune system was becoming weaker at a faster rate. For the first time, I felt the emotional toll. While the number of scientists studying HIV-AIDS and searching for effective treatments had multiplied, the number of people dying from the disease was exploding as the infection decimated immune systems. Even with all the precautions we knew we had to take, I was asking Pokey to risk her life to be my wife. And what would happen to Pokey if my health deteriorated?

Around this time, the local district superintendent of the United Methodist Church approached me about pastoring a small church in our area. The church, an older congregation, was on its last legs, but the denomination's administrators wanted it to die with dignity. Only a few short years since my first youth sermon, I was now stepping into a pastoral position where the future of the church depended on how God might work through my ministry. Even if the church was heading into a final transition, I believed it could still be a community where people knew they belonged. The job offered a small salary and housing—and most important, health insurance for both Pokey and me.

We set our wedding date for a few weeks later.

After our wedding, Pokey and I spent two years devoted to the people and ministries of that small church. Although the church did close a few years later, as the district superintendent expected, our sojourn there was rich in outreach and relationships. Perhaps the biggest imprint the experience made on me was that I began to think of pastoral ministry, rather than law, as a career.

Though Pokey and I were moving forward in planning a life together, we had some concerns. My blood work showed continued decline in my immune system, and I still had not found a specialist to guide me through the disease. And moving to North Carolina to attend seminary at Duke would mean once again looking for a job that included health benefits. Even as we wanted to follow where we believed God was leading, we faced a season of uncertainty when fear and doubt could easily take root.

Then I received an offer to be an assistant pastor at a church in Raleigh—with benefits—and I met Dr. Nancy Tatum. Following the health of a person living with HIV requires a doctor to spend considerable time and have considerable knowledge about the disease. Like me, many patients spend a long time looking for a doctor willing to take them on in a caring and supportive way, rather than a coldly dismissive manner.

Nancy was more than a doctor; she was my friend. She helped stabilize my condition from a medical point of view, but she also filled me with hope for fighting the disease, rather than fearing it. As I prepared to move to North Carolina, Nancy helped me connect with physicians there to care not just for my HIV but for all my medical issues.

Pokey shared my brokenness in intimate ways. It was healing to have her at my side and to have her family not turn away from me. Dr. Nancy was also beside me in my brokenness. I was definitely looking "through a glass darkly" in those days. I was sure of some things—like Pokey's love and my calling to be a pastor—but the shape of the future was still vague. Even as I continued my education and planned for a meaningful future, I didn't know what would happen. I carried in my body, a broken vessel, daily reminders that I need people to walk life's path alongside me. Being acutely aware of my own need perpetually kept before me the question of how I might come alongside others. Even if I hadn't become a pastor, these truths would have shaped my life.

COMMUNITY CARES

Our job is to make the person next to us look good. We're in this together. You help me live well, and I help you live well. When we grasp our shared humanity, rather than resisting it, the mirror becomes less dim. We begin to cast light on questions of health and health care.

When we are called to be people of faith, the first thing we think about is our relationship with God. Perhaps we develop habits of prayer and seeking God's presence. We crave that connection with the divine and marvel that humans can enter a conversation with the divine.

Too many of us stop there. But faith goes deeper and becomes more personal.

The more we are in relationship with the divine, the more the divine affects our humanity. We think differently. We speak differently. We find different values. Faith becomes a fundamental system that helps us understand the framework of who we are and what we've been called to do.

Faith goes deeper yet.

As being in relationship with the divine changes our experience of our own humanity, it also affects how we relate to other people—how we are in community with others. The divine affects our understanding of ourselves. We can be more truthful about our brokenness, our limits. And in the process the divine shapes us for a conversation about who we are and who we can be in relationship to others. Perhaps we learn to give the benefit of the doubt. Perhaps we are slower to speak. Perhaps we begin to walk in another's shoes.

Faith is transformative. The more we are in relationship with the divine, the crisper our sense of our own identity and the healthier our relationships with others will be. The natural output of being in relationship with God is that we are ready to see the world differently.

I have a friend who makes tapestries, a process I know little about. When she invited me to visit her studio, the first thing I saw when I walked in was the back of the tapestry she was working on. Shreds of thread were knotted and dangling, and the whole thing looked horrible. No way was I going to tell my friend she was a terrible tapestry maker!

Nevertheless, she discerned the thought in my expression.

"You're looking at it from the back," she said.

When she turned it around, I looked at one of the most beautiful things I've ever seen.

Faith turns the tapestry around. We may not always see the tapestry from the good side, but faith allows us to know that something beautiful awaits us. Even the knotted, tangled, hanging threads we see during seasons of pain and suffering prepare us to be part of creating goodness and beauty in our communities.

Our God, the world moves in a rhythm that we follow because we are told in so many ways what and how to think and feel. But you require us only to be still and know that you are God. Let the needs of love, compassion, and justice rule our day and not the things that matter not. Amen.

4

HELP MY UNBELIEF

*When we embrace uncertainty,
even doubt is a resource.*

Here's Scott:

One of my early patients was a woman about four feet eleven inches tall, bouncing off the walls because of the severity of her bipolar disorder. When we met, she crushed my hand in hers and said, "Hi, my name is Tiger."

Tiger had every problem imaginable that comes with substance abuse and mental illness, but something about her was endearing. I would see Tiger every couple of weeks. Sometimes her mood was elevated and sometimes it was subdued. Invariably, though, her circumstances were on the down and out. On several occasions

Tiger convinced me to find her a place to live or solve some other challenge of daily existence. Periodically her family would ask me to lead an intervention, which consistently ended with Tiger cussing me out.

And then she'd be back on the street.

Years later, Tiger was hit by a car. Even now I don't know what happened. For the last ten years of her life, Tiger was in a wheelchair. I would see her on the street, and she would chase me down in her chair. Whether she really could not walk or it was just one more con, I was never sure. But she got a lot of people trying to help her. They called themselves Team Tiger and did whatever they could to keep her functioning, until she dropped dead in her early fifties.

There have been a lot of Tigers in my life as a physician, a lot of people with complex needs, living with conditions most of us cannot imagine. Could I always be certain I was doing the right thing for Tiger? No. But I'm certain I was trying to act with compassion, and I learned a great deal about how *not* to do things by dealing with Tiger.

We live with uncertainty in everything we do every day. It's sort of the nature of practicing medicine to be unsure. I used to try, much more than I do now, to be up front and straightforward with patients and tell them I wasn't really sure about something. What I found out was that when I said that, more times than not, rather than a patient appreciating that I am just another human being giving the best I can offer and being honest about it, the person's attitude would be, "Well, I'm going to a doctor who is sure what he is doing!"

And yet, the fact of the matter is that in probably everything in life we operate with uncertainty. When we do anything that causes change in our lives, we're never absolutely sure. We get married, have kids, buy a new house, or change jobs. We do this or that. We're never quite sure. And then in issues of faith, we all want somebody to prove to us the existence of God, to prove to us those things that matter about faith. Yet, even in those things that are the closest to us, we can never be sure.

Where does that leave us? Hopefully, it leaves us with the belief that at some point we have to develop a sense of trust in our own abilities, in our friends, in God, in the belief that faith does matter. Trust is a very scary thing. I want to be sure about every step I take, but I rarely am. We need to be forgiving of each other, because there's no certainty in anything that we do. By the same token, we need to be more willing to trust each other because there is so little certainty in all that we do. •

Who among us can say we live without doubt?

Doubt in our own actions. Doubt in the decisions others make for or about us. Doubt in our parenting choices. Doubt about our major purchases. Doubt whether what we've always thought to be true really is true.

Doubt has value in our lives. It even has value in our faith. Doubt is not the opposite of faith, not by a long shot. If we wait for absolute certainty, we might never step out with a bold spirit to get something done—in our lives or in our communities.

I could have lived mired in doubt that I would see my twenty-first birthday. Statistically, it was improbable. I chose to believe that whatever happened, God would be present. While I had no certainty about anything, and plenty of reason to doubt, faith allowed me to embrace doubt as a part of my life and nevertheless take the next step that made sense. Perhaps this is what allowed me to hear the story of the Church Health Center and conclude that despite all the things that could go wrong along the way, it made perfect sense for Scott to believe the Center would succeed.

Scott was new and unknown to Memphis, but the prevailing mind-set was that if you care about Memphis, then Memphis will care about you. He came with youthful energy and enthusiasm to grab hold of one corner of a huge problem and not let go until he started to see progress. People were able to look past the ways he was rough around the edges and inexperienced with bureaucracy. Instead, they imagined possibility.

The possibility of helping thousands of people who were slipping through the cracks in one of the poorest cities in America.

The possibility for Memphis to be a better place to live no matter what your economic status.

The possibility for a city to care about people living at the edges.

The possibility for a professional community that would give back.

The possibility for people of all financial brackets to reach into their pockets and be generous.

Nothing was certain, but everything was possible.

Decision Points

I remember well one of my course-changing encounters with uncertainty on my way to becoming a United Methodist minister. Faith, health, and doubt jockeyed for top billing. I was still sorting out how all three could be true in one life.

During my second year of seminary at Duke, I began moving toward ordination. A routine health review as part of the process caught me off guard. Until then, I had regarded my HIV status as private, and I was in control of the situations in which I revealed I was HIV-positive. Now I had to provide this information in writing to the Board of Ministry.

The only alternative was backing away from the idea of being a pastor with traditional credentials. If I had known when Reverend Walley first took me on as his assistant, or when I pastored the church in decline, that someday I would stare at this question and feel my heart thicken, would I have stayed the course with studying law? By my second year at Duke, I was in pretty deep. I had arranged my life—and Pokey's—around the idea of preparing for a professional career in the church.

I could have kept that information private and abandoned the pursuit of ordination. After all, if they were asking health questions on the paperwork, that meant health questions could be a factor in accepting me for ordination. They might turn me down, and I would have revealed my HIV status to a group of strangers for nothing.

We don't always know what will happen after a decision, but we move forward. That's what I mean by embracing doubt as a part of the experience of faith.

Word spread quickly. I became the subject of telephone calls and special meetings. I was the first person with HIV to seek ordination in the United Methodist Church, and my application raised questions the Board of Ministry had never had to ask before. Despite all the furtive conversations, the process moved ahead.

The day came for my ordination interview. This is a stressful event for most candidates, but fretting over how people might respond to my complex health issues heightened my angst.

After routine questions about theology and my sense of call to pastoral ministry, someone finally asked the question that had been filling more and more space in the room since I entered.

"How will your health affect your ministry?"

I answered the best way I could, explaining my intention to do everything I could to take care of myself, just as a pastor with any other health issue would do.

More deliberations followed, both official and unofficial. My moral character was never in question. My theology was never in question. My gifts for ministry were never doubted. Even my call to the ministry was affirmed. It came down to whether the board would decline to ordain me because of a virus in my blood.

And would a church accept me if they knew I was HIV-positive? Although I had served in several churches by this time, there had been no reason to disclose my HIV status. Going forward, though, this information would be available to congregations. Would I somehow miss the calling of God for my life because I had a particular illness?

In the Methodist system, if you are accepted for the ministry, the regional conference that ordains you is obligated to place you in a church. I understood that alongside their faith in my calling and abilities, the Board of Ministry wrestled with doubts about whether they could uphold their end of the bargain.

The process of being appointed to a church brought reluctance, rejections, and downright threats of what would happen if a bishop appointed me to a particular congregation. It also brought multiple job offers, and Pokey and I were able to choose the one that seemed right for us at the time. I had several offers from people who knew me well. I could have continued at the church in Raleigh, for instance, but Pokey and I decided we needed to be closer to our families.

Over the next years, I served in several congregations and was involved in planting new churches. Some were places of affirmation and acceptance, but I knew that the specter of prejudice, fear, and ignorance could be just around the corner at any time.

In 2011, I arrived in Memphis to be senior pastor of a large United Methodist congregation. By this time I had written and spoken publicly about HIV many times and had lived with HIV for twenty-five years. My story is not one of defeat, but of joy and love and fulfillment. It binds together faith and health in spite of doubt. Every day I have opportunity to reflect on what healing means, how I can experience it, and how I can share it with others.

Because Scott was from Atlanta, he was ordained in the conference that served that region. When he moved to Memphis and had the opportunity to serve on the staff of St. John's as an associate to Frank McRae—"the one good white man"—the arrangement hinged on being able to transfer his ordination to the conference that Memphis was part of.

The Board of Ministry had a key question for Scott as they did for me: If the idea for the Church Health Center fails, then what?

What they were really saying was, "We'll be stuck with you if this doesn't work out."

Scott remembers, "I thought, *Would that really be such a bad thing?*"

He swallowed that reply and said something more politely convincing, and his ordination was transferred.

This was not the first, nor the last, confluence of faith and doubt in the history of the Church Health Center.

By this time, the Church Health Center had a home, but the renovations wouldn't come cheap. We might think that the words *Church Health* should at least have some clarity among Christians. The Church Health Center is unabashedly linked to the church and it has a ministry of health, just as Jesus did. In reality, the clarity has not always proven true. Denominations can be incredibly wary of each other and miss so many opportunities to live out God's justice together.

Before Scott ever arrived in Memphis, Frank McRae felt the divide between himself as a downtown mainline United Methodist minister and Jimmy Latimer, the pastor of Central Church, a large evangelical nondenominational suburban church that was in its heyday at the time. Eventually this bothered Frank enough that he took the attitude of Abraham Lincoln, who once said, "I don't like that man. I must get to know him better." Frank went to Latimer's office to introduce himself, and Latimer kept him waiting for a long time. No one would have blamed Frank for giving up, leaving, and classifying Latimer as somebody he would never have anything in common with. Frank had plenty on his plate already. Why was he spending so much of his day doing something nobody expected him to do?

But he stayed. And eventually Jimmy Latimer came out to talk to him.

This story is a lesson in finding common ground and waiting for relationships to take root in soil riddled with doubt. Once they finally began talking, Frank and Jimmy hit it off at some level and got past reticence about their differences. The day came that Jimmy called Frank and said he had a church member who wanted to give a hundred thousand dollars to an inner-city ministry. He figured Frank would be the guy to point him toward the right project.

Theologically Frank and Jimmy were as opposite as anyone could be, but Jimmy understood that Frank knew the inner city. He preached every Sunday in the heart of Memphis, in an area climbing back from decline. Frank told Jimmy, "I've got a young man from Atlanta I want you to meet."

Frank, Jimmy, and Scott gathered at Leonard's Pit Barbeque, a place that has been serving barbeque in Memphis since 1922.

"Theologically," Scott says, "I wasn't any closer to Jimmy than Frank was, but meeting Jimmy underscored that I didn't have a monopoly on wanting to do something to make life better for the poor in Memphis."

However, even with Frank's reputation as an influential pastor and the desire of the donor to give substantial money to a good cause, the search for common ground was intense. Almost from the start it was clear that the Christian calling to heal could have wide-ranging interpretations, and St. John's and Central had to find common ground without drawing a line in the sand that required complete agreement.

Money is serious stuff, and a thousand new scams pop up every day, so the people from Central Church wanted assurance they were not going to be left holding the bag if things went badly. More doubt! They drew up a document specifying that if the Church Health Center did not reach sustainability, for any reason, the building Central Church funds had renovated would be sold and Central Church would get their money back right off the top, before a penny went to St. John's. To their credit, St. John's didn't balk, even though they had put in a similar amount of money to purchase the building in the first place. That agreement was in force for ten years. By then the Church Health Center was on solid ground.

Help My Unbelief

A story from Jesus's life comes to mind. A man brought his son to Jesus for healing and said, "I believe; help my unbelief!" Doubt and faith and health were entwined in one story. For me that's a helpful reminder, and the history of the Church Health Center illustrates it well. Faith and health belong together, and doubt need not separate them.

For two and a half years in Florida I had lived with uncertainty about whether my work there would make a difference, whether it was a place where my family could thrive, whether I could face one more judgment about the kind of person I was based on the kind of disease I had, whether I could just make it through the day and get home to my wife and daughters. What was I doing there, in a place where I got beaten up nearly every day? I was in survival mode in Florida, a constant state of "fight or flight."

And it got to me.

I'd been a much better patient for most of my life. Florida changed that. Instead of being proactive about managing my own care, I didn't have the energy, physically or spiritually, and I let things go. I ignored warning signals—like pain in my ankle or the increase in my blood pressure.

People who live with chronic illness can either see the world as a dark place or view it with optimism. I had always chosen to be optimistic, but Florida shattered that. Taking care of myself physically seemed like too much on top of everything else. It became the thing I would do if I ever had time or energy—which was never, in those days. Rather than being the pilot of my own care ship because I had the tools and knowledge to know what to do, I waited for a crisis to happen. Then I would deal with it.

For a long time I didn't realize how much the stress of my position in Florida had affected me, or that I was so tired of the level of vigilance my health conditions required that I had checked out of the process. Faith and health and doubt were starting to come apart at the seams rather than being knit together in the way they were in the father's encounter with Jesus when his son was ill.

After I got to Memphis I overheard something one of my daughters said to her friend. The other girl was fussing about stuff that her father wouldn't let her do. I suppose it was the usual father-daughter friction over independence and makeup and clothing and age-appropriate activities. I'm sure I've given my daughter enough boundaries that she could have engaged in the preadolescent whining about unreasonable fathers.

Instead, I heard her say, "I worry every day that my dad might not be here."

Every day.

My daughter has legitimate reason for this uncertainty that colors her days. She knows my health issues are complex and serious, and that I have to think about them every day. We are a family, and what affects me affects all of us. My wife and daughters live with my health status right along with me. As a father, though, I want to help my daughters see past the risks, including the risk that I might not be here, to a life secure in the belief that they will be all right. I want them to know that whatever happens, they have the capacity to live in fullness and exuberance, with anticipation and aspiration. Fear and doubt are not all there is.

COMMUNITY CARES

The overwhelming message of the Bible is "Don't be afraid!" This is not to scold us, but to hearten us. As pressing as our doubts can be, especially if we do not dare to voice them, fear does not describe who we are.

In the Gospel of Mark, right before the story of the father who wanted Jesus to heal his son, we read about Jesus with three of his followers on the mountaintop, where his clothes became "dazzling white" and Elijah and Moses from the Old Testament appeared in this bath of light to talk with Jesus. It's hard to imagine a higher spiritual moment! When they came down from the mountain to meet up with the rest of the disciples, they found religious leaders snickering at the inability of Jesus's followers to heal the boy with a demon. A crowd had gathered to watch the showdown. It was complete chaos. Jesus snapped, "How much longer must I put up with you?" And then he healed the boy.

Faith and doubt are two sides of the same coin. At any moment, in our humanity we can give ourselves over to either side at the same level. In the same day, in the same hour, in the same conversation, we experience both sides. My grandfather used to say that love and hate are two sides of the same coin, but you're not in trouble until you throw the coin away. You risk throwing away love along with hate.

A person experiencing faith has pushed doubt far enough away for a time to believe that what's on one side of the coin is more important than the other. This doesn't mean the coin will never turn to the other side. Doubt creeps up as a reminder that we're human and we don't know everything, but it's gloriously a reminder that we're dealing in issues of faith and we're getting there most of the time. Even Jesus saw this reality unfold in that moment among the bickering crowd.

I was in a doctoral program at the same time as another man who was studying statistics. He researched the statistics of certain probabilities—flipping cards or coins, for instance—and discovered that strict fifty-fifty probability does not exist. If you flip a coin a hundred times, it won't land heads up exactly half the time. Each time you flip, some small factor affects what will happen and tilts the odds in one direction or another. These influencing factors may be so small they are not evident at first. Faith and doubt work the same way. Even when we trust, we endure doubt. We don't overcome doubt with a big, visible change so much as it takes just a little bit more faith, a little more trust, a little more trying to see the faith side of the coin. But if we hold on to the coin, we'll move toward hope.

On the other side of fear is hope, and that is the land where God means for us to live in health and well-being. We can help each other with the plea of "Help my unbelief!"

God of all, no matter how hard we try to be you, we see clearly our limitation. Some days we see the path, and then we step in a ditch. Remind us that you are our shepherd. Take our hand and lead us, Lord.

5

TEACH US TO SHARE

Let's open our hands and see what spills out.

Scott has an overflowing river of stories about patients. Here's one about a stunning gift that helped him care for his patients in the early days of the Church Health Center.

"He's insisting on seeing 'Scott.'"

Kim, the front-desk receptionist, presented the request, which could not have come at a worse time. It was December 23, and I was our only doctor. Everyone wanted to be well for Christmas. I had already seen more than forty patients, and the waiting room was still full.

"Does he have an appointment?" I asked.

"No. I don't remember him, and his name is not in the computer. He just keeps saying he wants to see Scott."

Knowing that I only needed to walk to the other side of the door and I could find out what the stranger wanted, I decided to get it over with. Wearing old blue jeans and a plaid shirt, and unshaven for several days, he hovered at the front desk.

When he saw my white coat, he turned to me and abruptly said, "Are you Scott?"

"Yes, sir, I am. How can I help you?"

"Can we go in the back?"

I had no idea what he wanted, but I did not think he was dangerous. The lab was the only room not occupied by a patient, so we went in there. The man gave me his name, but it meant nothing to me.

"I hear you do good work," he said, handing me an envelope. "If I ever hear my name associated with you, you will never hear from me again. Is that understood?"

"Yes, sir."

He shook my hand again. "Merry Christmas."

And he left.

The nurse gave me a look that said, *Don't you know you have patients waiting?* I did know, but I took another moment to open the envelope.

It contained a personal check for a hundred thousand dollars. When we were just starting out, that was nearly a third of our operating budget.

I ran to the front desk. "Kim! Did he tell you anything about himself?"

"No, he just wanted to see you. He seemed like a lot of our homeless guys, so I tried to be as nice as I knew to be."

Of course she did. That was Kim.

With a check for a hundred thousand dollars burning a hole in my pocket, I finished seeing patients.

That night I could think only of Kim treating him like another homeless man. For all she knew, that's what he was. But I had his name, so the next day I made some calls and learned he had a reputation for eccentricity that rivaled Howard Hughes.

Over the next ten years, the week before Christmas he or one of his sons would show up to drop off a check. There was never any conversation. I drove to his home one time with a small present that he clearly wasn't interested in.

Then one Christmas the check didn't come. And that was it. I knew he moved, but I don't know what else might have changed.

I do know that his unexpected generosity made it crystal clear to me that every homeless man is to be treated as if he is about to hand us a check for a hundred thousand dollars. It has never happened again that someone who looks like a bum handed me a large check, so that is not the point. His generosity taught me that everyone who walks through our door should be treated as though the person's value is greater than we could ever imagine. We begin with that assumption, and then from there we do the best we can to help. •

A new church in a new city gave me a fresh start on ministry, but it was not an instant cure for years of neglected self-care in body and spirit. Scott was one of the first people to recognize I was headed for trouble, and it was soon clear I needed vigorous care. Some of the treatments ahead of me meant I would be susceptible to side effects that would leave me unwell for days at a time in the short term while pursuing long-term benefits. I did not have cancer, but forty-eight weeks of chemotherapy was part of an aggressive plan to battle HIV and get my health back under control. This prospect was overwhelming. I was still fairly new to the congregation. The church knew I had serious chronic health issues and welcomed me anyway, but would getting sick so soon push on their generosity too hard?

The opposite happened.

Illness in any household affects everyone who lives there, not just the person who is ill. Routines change, and time for ordinary tasks, like meals, seems to evaporate. The people at church understood this, and an adult Sunday school class passed around a sign-up sheet to make sure my family was well fed. The staff and church leaders agreed on a plan that allowed me to be in the pulpit and continue to lead while recognizing that for a season I would have to step back from certain responsibilities. Other staff shifted their duties to cover pastoral work I might not be able to manage. And when a staff person had trouble juggling ongoing ministry at a retirement home and filling in for me at the same time, another Sunday school class took over at the retirement home to free up the staff person.

The church saw my illness as an opportunity to live out what it preaches Sunday to Sunday. After what happened in Florida, I had almost forgotten how gracious and caring people could be.

I had expected the least from those around me, but I was swept up in a deluge of generosity. While the church knew of my health conditions, I doubt they expected to be tested with a protracted care plan that forced me to make difficult choices. The church could have left me isolated in my illness. Instead they were companions in tangible ways.

Their generosity was a healing balm straight out of Gilead.

The greatest contribution you can make may be the thing you least expect. I learned that we can do what God calls us to do, but we don't have to do everything. I could step back and others would step up. We're all related. We can do more together. We're not supposed to be by ourselves. I've only begun to process what being reliant and dependent on other people really means to me. We are completely interdependent to become the healing and hope that God asks us to proclaim. Little of that has to do with the words we speak.

What the church gave me causes me to reflect on how we have opportunity to be generous companions with others on the journey toward health and wellness. And Scott's generosity toward me, when I hardly acknowledged my own need because of trauma in my life, goaded me to lift my eyes and see the gift that the Church Health Center has been to Memphis. Learning about the organization, and the provisions from donors large and small that have made it possible, has been eye-opening when it comes to understanding a community's power to change health.

Some of the stories from the beginning of the Church Health Center are priceless illustrations of a community banding together to share the resources that are right there in their own hands. If we open our hands, we might be surprised what we have to offer each other.

Chipping at the Challenge

Dick Trappier, a banker, sat on the board of the Plough Foundation. Abe Plough was a Memphis-area entrepreneur with a pharmaceutical empire that included St. Joseph children's aspirin, Dr. Scholl's products, and Maybelline cosmetics. When he died in 1984, he left his money to the Plough Foundation, which was headed by his daughter, Jocelyn Rudner. When Dick recommended Scott to Jocelyn, she consulted her son-in-law, John Eisenberg, who later led a prominent Washington-based research group and had plenty of smarts. Jocelyn wanted to know if it was possible Scott could actually persuade doctors to volunteer for a place like the Church Health Center.

"I doubt it," John said, "but why not give him a chance?"

So the first large gift the Church Health Center received for its operating budget came from a Jewish family foundation.

And it wasn't just about the money—or the fact that the Plough Foundation had a lot of money and Scott had nothing to put toward his cause, though that certainly was true.

The Plough Foundation represented a decades-long mission of supporting causes in and around Memphis that make people's lives better. They saw that Scott was trying to do the same thing.

Scott chipped away at the gap in his operating budget one request at a time. "I've always been good at screwing up my courage and knocking on the door," he says, "and doors have opened enough times to teach me to gamble on the next one and try again."

Part of being too young and dumb to know that what he wanted to do couldn't be done was that Scott lowballed the financial requests. Ten thousand dollars seemed like a small fortune to him, but the truth was that in some of his fundraising he should have added a zero or two, and the people he spoke to would not have blinked.

Other requests were more hard fought.

As a lifelong Methodist and an ordained Methodist minister, naturally he hoped the Methodist hospital would want to help. He was avid about healing and clueless about bureaucracy. He says, "That was probably one of my most Pollyanna moments. Students in medical school and residency focus on learning to be good doctors. How administrators make decisions for allocating resources is not part of the curriculum. Most doctors never understand the process."

Scott knew that the Methodist hospital was owned by three conferences of the United Methodist Church: the Memphis conference, the Arkansas conference, and the Mississippi conference. Bishops from all three conferences sat on the board of directors for the hospital. It made perfect sense to him that they would want to support a young Methodist minister trying to do, as both a pastor and a doctor, what John Wesley, founder of Methodism did.

What Scott didn't understand at the time, but does now, is that in 1986 the Methodist hospital had a strong corporate culture with questionable commitment to being the true faith-based organization it is today. It was a courageous move by Bob Howerton, senior vice president of health-and-wellness ministries, to take on finding the money Scott sought within the existing system. Nobody on the health-and-welfare side of hospital operations had ever asked for anything related to taking care of patients, which the Church Health Center would do.

Bob understood the call of John Wesley to take care of poor people when they got sick. Theoretically, he was in a position to take a proposal to the board of directors. But in most corporate cultures, if the CEO is not enthusiastic about a project before it formally comes to the board, it will sink like a loose anchor. At that point in time, the CEO of the hospital wasn't inclined to put his energy into caring for poor people. His job was to figure out how to keep the hospital afloat in a city where the Methodists were the weak link in the health care chain. The Baptists dominated, and the Catholics had two hospitals. The Med, the city-owned regional hospital, saw a large volume of patients, many of them low-income. But the Methodists? They were an afterthought for most of the medical professionals, or even patients, in Memphis. The best doctors didn't seek out affiliation with the Methodist system, and if the hospital was going to survive, that had to change. The CEO was trying to expand market share to try to make Methodist a player. The hospital's system wasn't designed to take care of poor people unless they showed up in the emergency room and could not be turned away.

Scott says, "I didn't understand these dynamics, or the fact that Bob was sticking his neck out and risking his job by taking on a cause like the Church Health Center. I would get frustrated because nothing seemed to be happening. Bob would assure me he was working on it. I would wait some more, see nothing happen, and get frustrated all over again."

A gift of a hundred thousand dollars from Methodist would mean the doors of the Church Health Center could open, but the wait seemed interminable.

One of the obstacles Bob ran into was doctors who didn't believe the focus of the Church Health Center truly would be on caring for the working uninsured. They defaulted to concluding that the Church Health Center would instead treat patients who were—or could be—paying patients at doctors' offices in the Methodist system. In their eyes, this essentially meant that Bob was asking them to support the competition. Doctors were independent contractors. Building a practice was a cutthroat endeavor, so why should they help Scott with his?

One influential doctor turned the tide. Dr. Charles Clarke was respected within the Methodist system, weak as it was compared to other hospitals in Memphis. Head of their medical systems, Charlie became convinced that supporting the Church Health Center was a good thing. Scott remained outside this process—which he later learned included a series of contentious encounters—but the outcome was that Charlie uncovered doctors who were willing to endorse the work of the center.

Scott recalls, "After a protracted eighteen-month process of breaking down opposition and misconception, the final 'ask' turned out to be much smoother than I anticipated. To me a hundred thousand dollars was one-third of the Church Health Center's annual budget. To the CEO, however, it was 'only' a hundred thousand. Compared to the entire budget of the hospital, it was not a significant amount to approve. Everything is relative."

The CEO said yes.

Scott was close to giddy at this point. With funds committed to cover two-thirds of the first year's operating budget, he could open the Church Health Center and begin seeing patients while he and his growing team of collaborators figured out where to get the rest of the money.

Scott would be the first to say he is an atrocious golfer, especially thirty years ago, but he will always golf for the good of the Church Health Center. He says, "The stereotypes about game-changing deals being done on the golf course have some truth to them. It's a way to meet people who can potentially write big checks, and it probably doesn't hurt if they win."

Larry Papasan, head of Memphis Light, Gas, and Water at the time Scott arrived in Memphis, arranged a golf outing with Jack Blair, who was a high-ranking executive at Smith & Nephew, a global orthopedic device maker. The three of them had lunch at the country club—Scott's first time to golf there. Then, on the first tee, in the middle of his backswing, Scott heard Jack and Larry start to laugh. It's easy to imagine how unnerving that would be if you're already self-conscious—and Scott was. He proceeded to hit his ball into the tennis courts, which, given the layout of the course, would be an incredibly difficult thing to accomplish if you set out to do it on purpose. I can just feel the flush that would pink up my own face if that happened to me.

Larry was straight-faced and confessed they were not laughing at Scott's swing. Jack had just asked Larry, "How much is this round of golf going to cost me?"

For several years after that, Smith & Nephew funded a significant portion of Scott's salary. Jack became a person who helped the Church Health Center raise money every year through a Golfing for Dollars event. Eventually the relationship came full circle in another dimension when Scott needed a joint replacement and ended up with a Smith & Nephew device in his own body.

Money keeps the lights on and the staff paid, but it wasn't everything the Church Health Center needed. What about volunteer doctors? What about connecting with the patients who needed them but did not know the center existed?

Gary Shorb was CEO of The Med, the region's public hospital. Trained as an engineer, Gary had been in the U.S. Navy on the staff of an admiral. He came to Memphis to work for Exxon, but didn't care much for the job. When he saw an opening for a vice president position at The Med, he applied. Within a few years, he became CEO. He wasn't much older than Scott was at the time. "Despite his title," Scott says, "talking to him about my grand vision wasn't daunting."

"Can you help me?" That's what it came down to—asking that simple question.

Gary wanted to help financially, and for the first three years after the Church Health Center opened, The Med underwrote about half of the employee salaries. But Gary also knew Scott needed to connect with the patient base the Center targeted. Scott explains, "The Church Health Center was not about raising money, but about helping people. I was working in a health-department clinic, so I knew the underserved patient population spilled out of every corner of Memphis. The challenge was not so much attracting patients to build a practice, but reaching the patients who needed us but didn't know we were there. Gary was in a unique position to help us do that."

The Med had a steady stream of low-income patients coming through their emergency department with nonemergency issues. They simply had no medical home, no doctor to see on a regular, preventive basis. If they got sick, even with something relatively minor, they went to the emergency department. These were the people the Church Health Center could serve by providing a primary care medical home. Gary widened the discussion to include

Dr. Art Kellerman, head of emergency services. They came up with names and addresses of two thousand patients who had used the emergency department for nonemergency care. Art and Gary crafted a letter and mailed an introduction to the Church Health Center.

That letter brought the first patients on opening day. After that, word of mouth took over.

When I hear pieces of the Church Health Center's history like this one, it underscores for me both the need for a place like the Church Health Center and what happens when people in a community come together to offer what they have, whether it's funding, a mailing list, professional expertise, or plain old hard work.

Willing Hearts, Capable Hands

As a pastor, I've known for years that the income that comes in through the offering plates (or online giving these days) is not the true picture of what people of faith give to their communities. Even a large church with a staff of pastors needs people to engage in practical ways to carry out the church's mission. That happens through volunteers.

One year I was in Mexico with a team building houses for two families. One family with two children depended on the father's income alone, and in the other both parents worked. As it turned out, the father was able to get some time off work so his entire family could help build their new home. In the other family, the parents were not able to leave their jobs. When each house was finished, we held a dedication where everyone who worked on the house held the key for a moment and could say something or pray. At the end of the circle, the family received the key. The husband and wife who were not able to work much on their house spoke with a sense of being "less than" the rest of the team, while the family who was there every day to help build their home spoke as confident members of the team.

As I listened to the difference in the ways they spoke, it occurred to me that when we volunteer and do good work, the ownership we have is a key factor in how we serve, but it also defines the depth of what we experience. If we do something because it seems like the right thing to do, that's good. The result will meet a need. But if we do it because we are serving together and building some-thing alongside each other, then we are doing life together. We're not doing something *for* someone at a distance but *with* someone, experiencing everything they experience.

On another occasion I walked up to three men who were painting walls of exterior siding. I asked the first man what he was doing, and he said he was painting. Short and to the point. The second person said he was "painting a wall to go on a house." A little more information, but still impersonal. The third man said he was "building a home for a friend of mine."

All three were doing the same activity, but each countenance was different because they saw what they were doing differently.

The work that can be accomplished in the faith community—and *by* the faith community—when everyone brings their gifts to the table is a measure of the health of the congregation. I've seen this truth played out in churches, and now I've seen it at work in the story of the Church Health Center. Even with all of my expe-rience, hearing stories of volunteers at the Church Health Center inspires me every time.

Dr. Pat Wall, who had a forty-five-year career in medical educa-tion in Memphis, was the first chair of the Church Health Center's board. He knew every doctor in Memphis, and he had an effective way of saying, "You're going to volunteer at the Church Health Center." One doctor at a time, they built a volunteer network that staffed the clinic in the evenings and on Saturdays.

Once physicians understood the Church Health Center was not filching their patients, only one—just one—ever turned down the opportunity, when asked, to volunteer with the Church Health Center at least a few hours every few months. It's a remarkable testament to the reach and endurance of the Church Health Center in the community that today a thousand doctors volunteer. Some see the Church Health Center patients in their own offices, while others rotate in the evening and weekend clinics or subspecialty clinics.

Doctors sometimes come to the Church Health Center in unconventional ways. One surgeon turned up in a Porsche because he was ticketed for going about 120 miles an hour in that sleek, gorgeous car. The court assigned him to do community service, and he chose the Church Health Center and began coming on Thursday mornings. Five years later, long after his community service had ended, he was still coming. He could see a patient in the Church Health Center clinic and then schedule to do the needed surgery himself.

Scott has had several joint replacements, and his own orthopedist eventually got his entire practice involved with the Church Health Center.

One retired doctor decided to come a half day once a week, then every day, then full time well into his eighties.

Over time, the retired doctor phenomenon took hold. "Doctors retired from their practices and played golf," Scott says. "After about six months they would realize they were bored. That's when they called the Church Health Center to inquire about volunteering on a regular basis." The Church Health Center now has fifty-two subspecialty clinics staffed with volunteer retired physicians who are experts in specific conditions.

The Church Health Center's family practice has twelve paid providers, but the vast volunteer network of medical professionals is what enables the organization to provide specific kinds of care that would be out of reach for uninsured people with low incomes.

A health ministry like the Church Health Center needs doctors and nurses, but it also needs muscles, clerical help, gardeners, IT, and welcomers.

James Fisher was a volunteer fixture for twelve years at Church Health Wellness, an eighty-thousand–square-foot facility for exercise, health education, and community. Bothered by arthritis, he first came because his doctor recommended aquatic therapy, which Wellness offered. But it was not long before James added volunteering to his daily routine. He arrived at six in the morning and offered his broad grin and twinkling eyes to people who came to Wellness for exercise, support groups, and classes.

James also exercised alongside others and encouraged Wellness members in their goals. When they thought they could not run one more step or lift one more weight, he was there to assure them they could and to celebrate their victories.

Some people called James the "banana man." When he first started volunteering, he brought various foods and candies to share with people. A staff dietitian took him aside and reminded him that Wellness was a place where people were working toward better health. James began bringing bananas every day instead of candy.

Celeste volunteered at the Church Health Center twice as long as James. When she was widowed in 1986, Celeste wondered what she was going to do with all the energy, time, and love inside her. Because she had worked in a doctor's office for twelve years, Celeste thought she might be some help at the Church Health Center. She was there the day in 1987 when the first clinic opened. She stayed until she was past ninety years old. Over the years Celeste put together patient charts, checked children's hearing and vision, decorated for Christmas, photocopied patient charts for disability claims, worked in bookkeeping, and wrote birthday cards to mail to other volunteers.

James and Celeste understood what it means to roll up their sleeves and plunge in to do what needs doing. Calculating the number of lives they have touched over the years through volunteering is impossible, but their consistent presence is a reminder of the beauty of a serving community.

Organizations run on the generosity of volunteers, and it's not busywork. Capable volunteers free up trained staff to do what only they can do. Generosity brings a community together, and the result is immeasurably more than the sum of the parts. The Church Health Center has built a community that crisscrosses people from varying backgrounds who would otherwise never have any connection to each other.

And that's a beautiful thing.

COMMUNITY CARES

My cousin died from a drug overdose. Our mothers were sisters, and when she was a little girl, she would come and stay with us. She was ten years younger than I was, and when I was in my first year of seminary I stayed with her family for a time while I was taking some courses in the town where she lived. I got to see what a beautiful young woman she was becoming. Somewhere around the end of high school, however, she got involved with a man who introduced her to drugs. Later it was crystal meth. Again and again I watched her seem to do better and then drop off the end of the earth, until she finally died.

She came from a family with the means to help her, but fighting her addiction was still too hard. Imagine what it would be like for someone who had no means, no family, no place to turn except perhaps an under-resourced county health clinic.

My cousin was not the only person I knew who struggled with addiction. As a pastor, I've had people in my ministry involved with drugs, whether it was a hard-core user or a stay-at-home mom hooked on prescription painkillers. I've seen up close the need for better help for more people. This issue had been on my mind for many years, but I had trouble sorting out how the churches I worked with could do something that would make a significant impact.

In preparation for tile work on a tabletop, I went to one of the big home-improvement stores for their do-it-yourself learning session on working with tile. As I handled both whole tiles and broken pieces, I discovered that a mosaic of broken pieces looked even more beautiful than the whole tiles. Bringing the broken bits together created something new, something unique, something that reminded me once again that we are all broken people who need each other to find our wholeness.

But still I faced the question of what this might have to do with my work in a congregation.

Then I met Scott and began to understand the work of the Church Health Center. Here at last was a place we could trust to start a Mosaic ministry. Memphis ranked fifth among fifty metropolitan areas in the country in terms of addiction disorders. In 2010, one-fourth of the population of Memphis had some issue of addictive behavior. The need was clear, and I was grateful to find a partner organization that had established trust, credibility, and competency within the community.

Faith expresses itself in generosity because in practical terms, resources are language. How we use our money is a language by which we ascribe value and transfer ownership based on ascribed value. Money is often a way that we say a person has accomplished something remarkable or has made it to the top. Faith challenges us by asking, "What language do you speak?"

Do we speak the language of self-centeredness? Or do we speak the language of generosity?

Faith makes us into something better than the world's standards, and generosity is a way of speaking that new language in a way the culture can hear.

The congregation I pastor is large and was already giving a quarter of its budget to missions. But in all that giving we had no relationship to the working poor in our own city, a place where health care and addiction recovery were out of reach for too many people.

So we started Mosaic.

In our own church, Mosaic relates to mental-health care for members or people associated with members. We make qualified help accessible. But we also wanted to provide care to people with fewer resources and more obstacles.

And nobody does that better than the Church Health Center.

Our funding for Mosaic expanded to supporting mental- and behavioral-health services to anyone in the city at the same level of care that one of our own members would receive. Whatever we did at Christ Church, we would also do for anyone in the city.

Resources are language. A congregation's budget or what they spend on serving is more than money. It's a statement to God and the community about what they value. And at Christ Church, we didn't want the community to think we didn't care about this glaring issue.

There's always a face. When I was trying to see how Mosaic could come to life, I saw my cousin's sweet face. Who would I trust with the care of someone I love? When we respond in ways that are personal, our generosity ceases to be a program or a budget item and instead becomes an investment of our faith. Let's open our hands and see what spills out.

Our God, we all depend on you for every breath we take, the joy we know, and the challenges we face. May your love be what drives our actions. Amen.

6

GOOD NEIGHBORS

We are not meant to live in isolation.

Here's Scott:

Rosemary, a regular patient with poorly controlled diabetes and a chronic mental illness, has more difficulties than most of the patients I see. A few years ago she had her right leg amputated, and then one day two years later, as soon as I walked in the room I could smell the foul odor of gangrene in her left foot. When I told her we would need to amputate her left leg, she asked me, "Has God abandoned me?"

She lived alone.

The utilities had been turned off in her apartment.

There was no one to help care for her, and she had no income.

What was I to say? I told her, "No, God has not abandoned you, because neither I nor the Church Health Center will abandon you. We will do all we can to help you through this ordeal."

For the moment, she was reassured, yet I knew we could not provide all that she needed. I wondered how she would cope when she returned to her home after the hospital discharged her. Who would take her there? How would she pay her heating bill in the coming winter? We could only do so much.

My sense of comfort was in knowing that my limitations are not God's. I see God's work in the patients who, despite the difficulties of poverty and life, still come and tell me they are in God's hands. •

When José arrived in Memphis, the plan was for him to work with his brother-in-law. Soon, though, José found himself very sick. Extremely jaundiced, he went to the emergency department at the hospital, where they told him he had hepatitis A, almost certainly contracted from a stranger who was very sick when they crossed the desert together and for whom José had offered what care he could under the circumstances. José would get better, but on top of feeling terrible physically, he also felt guilty that he was not able to help his brother-in-law. After all, that was why he came to Memphis. Later, he visited the Church Health Center, where Scott saw him. José had a horrible pain in his right hand and could not hold a hammer. He was young for the disease, but José had gout.

Scott told him to take the week off. José would have many years to work and repay his family for caring for him during his illness. José looked Scott in the eye and said, "Now that I know you are caring for me, I know I will get better." José had been a caring presence to the stranger in the desert. It seemed right that now he had found someone who would care for him.

America's First Hospital

Living with hemophilia and HIV, I've seen the insides of hospitals more than most people ever will. Tests. Admissions. Treatments. Emergencies. Specialists. Surgeries. No one goes to a hospital seeking warm fuzzies. We know they are generally clinical places trying to be efficient about clinical care.

Did you know that the first hospital in America has its roots in the concept of being good neighbors? Ben Franklin, famous for his pithy quotations, quirky inventions—including bifocal glasses we take for granted—and statesmanship, had a lot to do with it.

Between 1730 and 1776, shipping and trade with Europe brought droves of people to Philadelphia, many of them poor. In the middle of this period of rapid growth, Dr. Bond, a Quaker, wanted to care for the poor. He appealed to Franklin for help getting funding through the Pennsylvania Assembly. Franklin proposed that the Assembly provide two thousand British pounds if he was able to raise another two thousand British pounds from private donations. The politicians agreed, perhaps because they doubted he could do it. But Franklin raised this amount and more. As a result, America's first hospital opened in 1751 with the purpose "to care for the sick-poor and insane" who were wandering the streets of Philadelphia. The seal of the hospital featured a picture of the Good Samaritan and the words, "Take care of him and I will repay thee."

The first hospital in America—not even yet a nation—set the precedent for caring for the poor using financial help from good neighbors in both the public and private sectors—and on the foundation of a story Jesus told to help us see who our neighbors are. Near the time of his death in 1790 at the age of eighty-four, Franklin regarded the hospital as one of his most important achievements.

What does it mean to be good neighbors when it comes to health care more than two hundred years after Benjamin Franklin established his hospital? Scott was about to find out, as he prepared to open the Church Health Center.

When it was time for the renovations of the building St. John's had purchased and Central Church had agreed to renovate, the architect's opinion was that enclosing the front porch was the only way they were going to get the square footage required to create enough exam rooms and still have space for a reasonable waiting area. Although the house dated to the 1920s, it was not deemed historic by any standard that would prevent the renovations. The problem was the nearest street corner, Peabody and Bellevue. The building was within a hundred feet of that corner, which meant it was within a hundred feet of Annesdale Park Historic District on the other side of the traffic light.

About a decade before Scott's arrival in Memphis, several historic districts began forming to halt encroaching commercialization of properties in historic sections of the city and generally to watch out for the welfare of the homes in these areas. So in 1987, residents of these neighborhoods were on high alert for proposed changes that might smirch the image of gracious historic living they had worked so hard to reclaim. The hundred-foot marker gave them the right to weigh in on whether any proposed land-use changes were "appropriate."

Eventually the Church Health Center needed the city council to approve enclosing the front porch. The Annesdale neighborhood association regularly met in the basement of St. John's, across the street from the house in question. People were up in arms about what Scott wanted to do, and a series of meetings ensued.

"Previous groups patted me on the back and told me how noble my ideas were," Scott says. "But instead of comparing me to Albert Schweitzer, this group pictured me as Attila the Hun. The tenor of these discussions was acrimonious and brimming with misinformation. Finally, in side conversations, I won over an elderly woman who lived a block from St. John's in Annesdale Park and was also a member of the church. As a crucial meeting approached, she was prepared to speak in favor of the Church Health Center. She was well liked and influential, so her willingness to endorse us could be the turning point we needed."

Frank McRae and Scott both arranged to be present at the meeting where association members would discuss the Church Health Center. Normally twenty or thirty people would meet and formulate an opinion about a question affecting the neighborhood. On the night enclosing the front porch was on the agenda, the fellowship hall at St. John's overflowed. Frank and Scott arrived a few minutes early and awaited the entrance of their star witness. The clock ticked toward starting time—and then past. Their well-respected representative had not shown up.

She was like the old E. F. Hutton commercials—everybody listened to her. They needed her to talk.

Frank called her, but she didn't answer her phone. Scott and Frank scrambled across the intersection and hustled to her nearby home to find out why she hadn't appeared. They could tell she was home. Lights were on and curtains were open. They had every reason to believe she was inside. When she didn't answer the door, they became concerned for her welfare and decided to break in.

They found her. She'd had a heart attack and died right before the time appointed for the meeting.

The night's agenda got called off because everyone loved this woman and the gathering was stunned by her death. When the Annesdale association convened again in another week or so, however, the conversation deteriorated rapidly.

Scott has often repeated one memorable statement made that night that summed up the sentiment in the room: "If we let this clinic open, young bucks will drop off their mothers and go thieving through the neighborhood."

How is dialogue even possible when minds have leaped to such an extreme conclusion? After two hours of debate, the association voted to formally oppose the petition for a special-use permit that would allow the Church Health Center to enclose the front porch. Only nine people voted on the Church Health Center's side. Scott was crushed.

Fortunately, his friends reminded him that this was not the vote that counted. Their next stop was the land-use control board. Regardless of what the people of Annesdale thought, the committee members mattered most. This was another occasion indelibly scratched into Scott's memory.

"When my friends and I arrived, we could hardly get in the door for the agitated crowd. Clearly the various historic-district associations had banded together for an impressive turnout. If numbers alone meant anything, we were sunk. Other than our own voices, no one present intended to speak on our behalf, and sure enough, no one did. Plenty of people made a grab for the microphone to speak their minds about how enclosing a front porch was going to lead to the downfall of one of Memphis's beloved neighborhoods.

"I gave my most impassioned explanation of how the Church Health Center would be good for Memphis without harming the residents of the historic districts, and fortunately the committee didn't find the young buck's argument persuasive. They recommended moving the question on to the city council for an official approval."

Scott then took a crash course in local politics, trying to explain to every city councilperson how the Church Health Center would help the neighborhood, not harm it.

"I had no idea what I was doing," he says. "I was a doctor and a minister, not a politician. No one ever told me that providing health care to the poor in the name of the church would require waging a political battle. 'Please, God, help them to make a wise decision' was my prayer every night as I went to bed but not to sleep."

He couldn't eat on the day of the vote. The stakes were bigger, and so was the crowd. Apparently his performance at the land-use meeting hadn't converted anyone from the neighborhood. The clear message was, "You'll never get city council approval."

Frank, Zeno (the architect), Ann (the attorney), and Scott walked in with a handful of supporters. Ann pointed to a chair and kindly but firmly suggested Scott sit down.

"You're not going to talk," she said. "Not one word."

The Church Health Center was Scott's baby. The idea of not talking to the people making a critical decision unnerved him, but he trusted Ann to have his back. He swallowed and agreed.

"Ann was a marvel to watch as she laid out the truths of the case with the splendid eloquence of a lawyer trained in persuasive speeches," Scott says. "This was the first time I heard her argue a case, and from that moment I knew I would always want her on my side."

"Have you explored other locations?" Florence, a city council-woman interrupted Ann.

"Yes, ma'am, we have, and we believe this is the best that is available."

Florence snapped, "Well, I don't want it in my neighborhood."

She lived almost two miles from the Church Health Center site—quite a distance from the project to claim it as her neighborhood. Scott's stomach churned, and he couldn't pay attention to the discussion.

Finally, after nearly three hours, the time came for the vote.

"All in favor say, 'Aye.' Those opposed say, 'No,'" instructed the council chair.

"Aye."

"Aye."

"Aye."

"No."

"Aye."

"Aye."

It passed.

The victory was bittersweet, though. Scott had permission to proceed with a ministry of health care for the working poor in what is historically the poorest major city in America, but it was becoming clear that skeptics were a formidable challenge.

Attitudes from the immediate neighborhood were only the beginning. Scott was soon to discover that the major hospital systems in Memphis didn't have a very neighborly relationship. With the help of influential physicians, interest grew steadily among individual doctors in helping the Church Health Center. But if a patient needed services from volunteer doctors who were not in the same system, the process got complicated.

Charlie Handorf, treasurer of the local medical society for many years, wanted everyone to believe he was a curmudgeon who wouldn't spend a dime of medical society money for anything he didn't deem essential. Charlie was also a pathologist, and Scott needed pathologists. Charlie got his entire practice to donate their time—in the Methodist system. The dilemma was that most of the doctors Scott met did not function in the Methodist system. This led to some ridiculous workarounds in order to take care of his patients.

For instance, Dr. Pagett, a member of St. John's, was a cancer surgeon in the Baptist system. If Scott saw a woman in the clinic who had a breast mass, he could send her to Dr. Pagett, who would gladly take the sample needed for a biopsy. Now Scott needed a pathologist to evaluate the sample. Dr. Handorf was ready to help, but how would the specimen get from a Baptist doctor to a Methodist doctor?

Dr. Pagett would do the biopsy, put the specimen in a jar, and hand it to the patient. The patient would carry it back to Scott, and he would get it to the Methodist pathologist. If Dr. Handorf or one of his associates determined that cancer was present in the sample cells, they would tell Scott, who would tell Dr. Pagett, who would proceed with surgery at the Baptist hospital.

Inefficient, to say the least. It was like living between two neighbors who don't speak to each other and coaxing them to cooperate on a fence everyone shares.

Today most of the major medical practices and facilities work with the Church Health Center in some way, and with each other. While they remain mindful of the needs of their own businesses, the Church Health Center has helped raise awareness of the needs of the uninsured or others living in the gaps that socioeconomic inequalities create. The Church Health Center has grown from being the suspect, unproven outsider to a leading insider other organizations are eager to work with. If I were to sketch out all the ways that Church Health Center is connected to businesses and organizations in Memphis, the end result would look like a tightly woven fabric. Good neighbor relationships have been a hallmark. Scott has always believed the community can do more by working together to enlarge their circles than by protecting their turf. The people who need the services of the Church Health Center are part of the community, and so are the people who make the services possible.

It breaks my heart to hear about people like Rosemary, who wondered if even God had abandoned her.

Good neighbors can do better than that.

Neighbors for the Community

One topic that Scott and I enjoy talking about from time to time is baseball. He's been a lifelong fan and has some great stories! One story, though, is bittersweet.

He was seven when his aunt married a pitcher for the Atlanta Crackers, the AAA affiliate of the St. Louis Cardinals. The next year Scott's new uncle was traded to the Milwaukee Braves, and Scott got on a plane in Atlanta by himself and flew to Milwaukee. When his aunt and uncle collected him, they went directly to a team party. Wide-eyed, Scott met Warren Spahn, Del Crandall, and, most important, Hank Aaron. No wonder he dreamed of a career in the big leagues. He rubbed shoulders with some of the best.

A few years later, Scott says, "God smiled on me when I was twelve and the Braves moved to Atlanta." He went to the Braves' first game in Atlanta Stadium in 1966. He also saw Sandy Koufax pitch a classic game against Tony Cloninger that summer. Over the years he defended the play of Hank Aaron to his next-door neighbor, who called Hank slow and lazy. At the time he didn't realize his neighbor was making stereotypically racial slurs.

In 1968, after Martin Luther King Jr. was killed in Memphis, civil rights issues exploded all over the South. Mayor Ivan Allen of Atlanta stood in a car and called for racial harmony, and the city heard his pleas. Dubbed "the City Too Busy to Hate," Atlanta became known as the Southern city that did not let race destroy it.

But a few years ago when Scott heard the Braves were moving from Atlanta to suburban Cobb County, he felt physically sick.

"I lived in Atlanta when MARTA, the city's transportation network, was created," he explains. "At the time, Cobb County voted *not* to fund having the rapid transit system enter the county. I remember people saying that MARTA stood for 'Moving Africans Rapidly Through Atlanta.'"

Despite the press releases stating that the move was a business decision in order to keep the team competitive, pure and simple, for Scott it's hard to ignore that the Braves consider their fan base to be in the county that refused MARTA because of racial bias.

He says, "The city that avoided letting race define it in the 1960s was now being redefined by a more insidious form of racial disparity—the one driven by race-related poverty. I've had more than one older patient tell me something like, 'I've never been treated so well by a white doctor.' Of course, I like confirmation that we have treated them with kindness and dignity. At the same time, it saddens me that for a person's entire lifetime, he or she has been treated as 'less than.' Whether I like it or not, I can't know what it's like to be black. I can't even understand what it's like to be poor. If I gave away everything I own and kept nothing for myself, I wouldn't truly be poor. Because of my education, I could excise myself from living poor at any moment I chose."

Good neighbors can do better than that.

Memphis and Atlanta are not the only cities that should be asking questions about how to be good neighbors. That's a question for all of us to consider.

The well-being of a community bears on the well-being of the individual. What might look like a business decision on the surface can have roots in inequality that was overt and rampant in the past and now manifests itself in more subtle—but just as dangerous—ways. When it comes to health, and to expressing our faith conviction of God's intention for wellness and healing, we have to see where we've come from in order to see where we need to go. Understanding how we've failed to be good neighbors in the past will make us better neighbors in the future.

COMMUNITY CARES

I hadn't been in Memphis very long before I knew that I wanted my congregation to be more involved with the Church Health Center. We had a lot to learn from the Church Health Center about being good neighbors, about living among the people we serve and experiencing life together as a community. It wasn't enough to be "benefactors" to "people in need."

We had to take the next step and learn to be good neighbors.

The church has been engaged with providing housing repair and helping to found an alternative school for at-risk students. But the thing I wanted to see is every person in the congregation engaged and bringing their gifts to the community table. Faith communities are not just supposed to create ministries that people can give money to or even to serve; we need to incubate opportunities for people to be using their gifts and understanding the potential of their contributions to make health happen in a community. It might be in the area of race relations. It might be a daycare for families in the neighborhood. It might be homing in on meeting basic physical needs. It might be providing transportation to a person who is older or has a disability and does not drive.

How can we be concerned about the health of our community?

It's a straightforward question. Sometimes we make it more complicated than it needs to be. It helps to have names and faces in front of us as we answer the question.

How can we help Joe and Betty, who are in our congregation, to be healthier so that they can go into the community and help it to be healthier?

While I am pastoring a large well-resourced church now, this has not always been the case. At one point I was a part-time pastor of a church with eleven people.

You read that right. Eleven.

I was pastor of another congregation at the same time, but I went out every Sunday morning and preached at eight o'clock to this group of eleven people. One member was sixty-two, but the others ranged in age from their seventies to their nineties. The question would come up: "What can we do? We've always been small."

"Look around," I told them. "What is just one thing you can do?"

They decided to work with a county school and collect school supplies into care packages that could go to families who needed them. As it turned out, one of the families they helped lived just across the street from the church in a trailer behind an old house that had burned out. One day the mother and two children walked across the street to say thank you for the supplies.

Two members of that aging congregation were retired carpenters. One room at a time, that little church of eleven senior citizens helped renovate the damaged house.

We are not meant to live in isolation. Being a good neighbor begins with simply looking around.

> *Our God, we are all so different, yet we are all the same. Forgive us when we hold those who are like us to a higher plane. Forgive us when we turn our backs to those who are different and claim our way as better. Hear our prayer for our broken world. Amen.*

7

THE EMPTY CHAIR

Everybody has a place at the table.

Here's Scott:

George was only fifty-one but obviously had seen a lot of miles. His weather-beaten face was cracked from decades of being in the sun working as a body man, hammering dents out of vehicles. After a heart attack in his early forties, he had to quit. Following a triple bypass operation he has never felt right—dizzy and unsteady on his feet. George kept trying to go back to work, but he couldn't. A few years later he applied for disability, but was turned down. Since then he had been living with his mother. "When you've worked all your life," he said, "it's hard to go back and live off your mother, but I didn't have any choice."

George's sister brought him to see me because he had fallen and broken his hand. When I felt his hand, it was ice cold. My first thought was that the fall had also damaged the blood supply to his hand, but he had good pulses. George said his hand had been cold ever since his heart surgery.

"That's why I can't work," he said.

I could see the problem.

I set to work putting a cast on the hand and said, "I'll do whatever I can to help you get disability. We need to figure out a few things, like why your hand is cold and why you keep falling."

"I'd be much obliged."

It was astonishing to me that no one had tried to help George in the nine years since his surgery. ·

My grandfather, who was a formative personality in my childhood, always kept an empty chair at the table. He lived on a farm. People were always stopping by, and he was always ready for them even if a meal was about to go on the table. That memory makes me think of the Jewish tradition of pouring a glass of wine for Elijah at the Seder meal or even setting a place for him, no matter how crowded the table is. In Jewish heritage, Elijah is the one who will announce that the messianic era of peace and well-being has begun, bringing an end to the exile and mourning of so much of Jewish history. Some synagogues also have a Chair of Elijah, which is empty except following the reading of the Torah, when a member of the community has the honor of holding the Torah and sitting in the chair. When this happens, the sacred text and tradition of the Torah fills the Chair of Elijah. Again, Elijah represents the peace and well-being that comes with the presence of God.

Wholeness and wellness are bigger than individual right. They are a necessity for the kind of world we want to create—a world that regards individuals with worth and dignity because God regards them that way.

Why does George feel so alone? Where is the community that can invite him to the table so he can know his worth in God's eyes?

Level Dignity

"I try to keep my chair lower than the patient's," Scott says, "and never to talk standing up while the patient is sitting down. It's inherently unequal."

I like this image of Scott's chair as much as I like the memory of my grandfather's empty chair or the expectation of God's presence in Elijah's empty chair. There's dignity in leveling the playing field even for the course of a conversation, and this opens up space for learning, for connecting, for seeing each other as human beings with a great deal in common in our experience of life, including our quest for the peace and well-being that comes from the presence of God in our lives.

In the South it's common to ask how someone is and get the response, "Fine and blessed." Scott and I have talked about how remarkable it is to hear this from people who clearly have difficult, complicated lives. They may be in poor health, they may have little money, they may have been taken advantage of by their family members, yet they will say they are "fine and blessed."

Mary, the mother of Jesus, considered herself fine and blessed when her life was on the brink of scandal. An angel visited with news that almost no one was going to believe—that she would be mother to the Son of God. Yet Mary said, "From now on all generations will call me blessed; for the Mighty One has done great things for me, and holy is his name" (Luke 1:48–49).

Mary had a peace with the world and knew God was present, saying, "He has brought down the powerful from their thrones, and lifted up the lowly; he has filled the hungry with good things, and sent the rich away empty" (Luke 1:52–53).

Scott reminds me that this is not only a metaphor about spirituality. "God definitely acts in our world in unexpected ways. God lifts up poor people. God lives with the poor. God's order reverses our systems, however profitable and well-oiled they might be. It is easy to treat poor people when they are sick without truly being engaged in their lives. One of the challenges of poverty medicine is realizing that you are capable of doing only so much. Poverty generates overwhelming needs."

What might happen, I wonder, in the world of health if more of us did our parts? What if we made room at our tables and heard the stories of people who live across the street or across town? How might we transform our communities into healthy places where everyone has a place at the table, and George would be cared for with dignity?

Scott tells a touching story about his father that illustrates the dignity that comes from listening to each other for more than cold, clinical information. In my mind it probes a needed question about how we can work together toward a whole, well society. Here it is:

· · · · · · · · In the spring of 1952, during the Korean War, my father was flying a small fighter plane off an aircraft carrier in the China Sea. Officially, U.S. forces were not supposed to be flying over North Korea, but he was on an assigned mission with a target to bomb. He flew very low, and anti-aircraft fire exploded around him. His plane was shot in hundreds of places, leaving him no option but to bail out.

When his parachute landed, my father knew he was in danger. As a twenty-two-year-old Navy officer, he had no intention of being captured. He was armed to the teeth, and when a truck rumbled toward him, he was prepared to fight. My father readied his handgun. Over the hill came a U.S. Marine. With his adrenaline on overload, my father's aim did not waver.

Calmly, the Marine said, "Give me your gun." My father turned it over.

Back on the aircraft carrier, officers debriefed him about the incident. After a few brief questions, someone asked, "What happened to your gun?"

"I don't remember," he replied.

Over the next few weeks, my father had several more interviews. He remembers, "I was asked over and over again about what happened to my gun, but no one ever asked what happened to *me*." After more than sixty years, my father's favorite song is still the Marine Corps hymn because a Marine rescued him, but he has never forgotten that no one asked about *him* on that day.

The truth is, we rarely ask about the other person and how he or she really feels. We are quick to tell our story. We seem to always believe that our point of view is more interesting, more important, and more meaningful than the person we are talking to. I find myself doing it. What is worse, I do it without realizing it. I hate it when I finally catch myself interrupting someone telling a story. It means I am not fully listening to what the person is saying.

My father rarely, in my presence, has told the story of being shot down. Whenever he has, I didn't care what happened to the gun. I cared about what happened to him. •

Scott and his wife, Mary, once went to see their friends Willard and Rita. This was toward the end of Willard's life, after he had developed thyroid cancer. There in the room was John Calipari and his wife, Ellen. Anyone who follows college basketball, especially in the South, knows John Calipari. Willard and Rita were big supporters of the University of Memphis, where John spent several years leading the Tigers to an impressive basketball record. As he said goodbye, John suggested they all have a prayer together.

"I was the only preacher in the room," Scott says. "But before I could open my mouth, John prayed the best bedside prayer I have ever heard. He'd thought about it. This obviously wasn't his first time."

In recent years Calipari has been overt about his personal faith, even in the media. His wife has been a Methodist all her life, and John worships with their family in a Methodist church. During the week, however, he attends Mass in a Catholic church nearly every morning. Calipari has more than five hundred college basketball wins on his record and has aggressively built winning teams at several schools. Yet in that room, he showed a different side than most people get to see. He leveled the field to a loving expression of dignity and care for someone in a vulnerable position.

People are complicated, but we share our humanity. Our various expressions of faith don't have to separate us nearly as much as they do. It's easy to make assumptions about people based on some small aspect that we observe. Often what we observe is superficial, and so are our assumptions. Or, we miss the opportunity to recognize the humanity we share because we get caught up in our own agendas.

Sadly, health is one of those places in our life together where we keep our distance. Because I am HIV-positive, I've known people—even before the open hostility in Florida—who weren't sure how to relate to me. Pity? Suspicion? Hesitancy? I've known people who wouldn't even agree to speak with me on the phone. I wish I could say it's different in the health care system, but I've experienced doctors who saw the science of my disease more than they saw me as a person. I've been to clinics where I was asked to use a separate entrance from patients who do not carry the HIV virus. I've known what it's like to live with the fear of being denied insurance, to have my life threatened by what could happen if I didn't have access to health care.

People who don't even know me make assumptions about the circumstances in my life that resulted in having a disease and about what kind of person I must be.

I cringe when I see this happening at a societal level. The truth is we are caught in cycles of prejudice and judgment. Why is that unmarried woman with three children having another one? If that man with his "Homeless. Anything Will Help" sign on the corner would try harder, he could get a job. That person ruined his life by drinking because he just wouldn't give it up. If she would get out of bed once in a while, maybe she wouldn't be so depressed. If that family was willing to move to a better neighborhood, their kids could go to a decent school. Why is she on disability when she looks perfectly fine to me?

These thoughts run through our minds, and we don't even glimpse the underlying truths that we are separating ourselves from suffering people, and in seeing them as "other" than what we are, we sacrifice their dignity on the altar of our self-righteousness. Then the conversation—if we dare to have it—crumbles into hostility about whose responsibility it is to help.

It's my responsibility to help.

It's yours.

It's *not* our responsibility to assign people to columns of *Deserving* and *Undeserving*. The truth is millions of people have far less control over the circumstances of their lives than we might think—children who go to school hungry, people living in poverty, lack of good schools, living in dangerous neighborhoods, lack of transportation, exposure to violence. And all these circumstances that sound social or economic affect their health and whether they receive care. We're wrong when we try to talk about health without also talking about these issues. Just wrong.

Grasping our shared humanity helps us embrace our shared dignity. I've seen that one truth change a person's health and well-being—my own.

I hear people of faith separating God's desire for all people to be whole and redeemed—healed—from any sense of obligation to participate in healing. Even worse is the tendency to blame people for their need for healing rather than recognize that we're all broken. We all need healing. In fact, our society and our world need healing.

There is no *us* and *them.*

It's different at the Church Health Center. The organization exists to serve the underserved, and the way they do it is to rediscover our shared humanity every day and extend dignity to one person at a time.

Listening to the stories.

Being advocates for the weak.

Promising companionship in scary times.

Welcoming people on the margins.

Loving without judgment.

Affirming the value of faith, no matter its form.

For the last few years, the Church Health Center has been involved with the Institute for Healthcare Improvement, an organization out of Boston that offers a framework for improving health care and a conversation at a global level. They call it the Triple Aim—to improve the patient experience of care, to improve the health of populations, and to do both of these while reducing the cost of health care. In an initiative called Healthy Shelby, Shelby County, Tennessee, became one of the first communities in the country to join IHI's "Triple Aim in a Region" community. Scott has been connected to IHI, and the model of integrated care that the Church Health Center uses garners wide interest.

I've always appreciated that Scott also points out another triple aim—from the book of Micah in the Old Testament: "He has told you, O mortal, what is good; and what does the LORD require of you but to do justice, and to love kindness, and to walk humbly with your God?" (Mic. 6:8).

"If we put the IHI Triple Aim alongside Micah's triple aim to do justice, love kindness, and walk humbly with God," Scott says, "what difference might it make in how we participate in our own health and the care of others? What would it really take for people of faith who embrace Micah's words to change the way we talk about health?"

That is a good question.

New Solutions

One of the most inspiring ways I've seen the Church Health Center do justice and love kindness is by initiating a plan that enables patients to see doctors all over Memphis. Not every patient eligible for services can come to the center's clinic, and neither can every doctor who wishes to volunteer services.

A few years after it opened, the Church Health Center successfully petitioned the state legislature to enact a law allowing it to offer the MEMPHIS Plan, an employer-sponsored health program that extends care to thousands of Memphis residents who otherwise would not have access to affordable services. This plan is a volunteer health care plan designed to serve uninsured workers whose earnings are near the minimum wage. Small businesses and the self-employed are eligible to participate in the MEMPHIS Plan. Employer and employee share low premiums for a covered worker and dependents. Individuals enrolled in the plan are assigned to primary care physicians who volunteer for the MEMPHIS Plan and see patients in their own practices. The plan provides many of the same benefits as traditional insurance, but because all the services are donated, it is not required to have the substantial financial reserves that insurance plans must maintain.

This idea is particularly inspiring to me, because Scott and his team took it all the way through the legislative process. A light-bulb went on, and they did what was necessary to keep it shining. People for whom health care was prohibitive, both in terms of cost and access, now were treated with dignity. And over the years, the data shows it's working. Participants in the MEMPHIS Plan have fewer hospitalizations and shorter stays than patients in a control group of another family practice that serves a similar population.

Not everyone thinks outside the box this way, and sometimes boxes collide, as they do in this story from Scott:

· · · · · · · · · I was seeing a patient when a staff member who worked for the MEMPHIS Plan paged me.

"Do you remember Mr. Sayers who we sent to the neurosurgery clinic?" she asked.

I had only a vague memory.

She gave me a name. "This doctor just called me and threatened to report us to the *Commercial Appeal* because we don't know that Mr. Sayers has multiple sclerosis and needs to see a neurologist and not a neurosurgeon. Why have we sent him to them? He went on and on like that. He wants you to call."

"Who is he?" I asked. "I've never heard his name."

"He says he's the head of neurosurgery."

I girded myself in courage and dialed the number. The doctor answered.

"How can I help you?" I said after introducing myself.

For a few seconds he was cordial. Then he let me have it. "This man has been suffering from MS since November, and y'all keep sending him to us. If I sent him to the Med, he would see a neurologist in a couple of hours, but you refuse to pay for the care he needs."

My heart was pounding by now. It was clear this doctor knew nothing about the Church Health Center.

"Let me tell you how our MEMPHIS Plan works," I said as calmly as I could. I described our network of volunteer providers. But even as I did this, I was more and more angry at his chewing me out. I knew I was crossing the line when I said, "I'm sorry we referred a patient to you with a problem you are not competent to deal with."

My voice quavered and I gulped for air as I tried to shift my tone. "Please send the patient to the Church Health Center now and I will make sure a neurologist sees him."

Now the doctor began to apologize for his attitude. "I'm sorry. I didn't know who you were. I thought I was dealing with an insurance company who was refusing to help the patient. I hope you will accept my apology."

"No problem," I said. "Just send Mr. Sayers over."

I wanted to sit and regroup, but the nurses had filled all my exam rooms with waiting patients. It was hard to walk into the next room and smile.

About an hour later, I came out of a room and there was a young doctor waiting to talk to me. He introduced himself and said, "After we hung up, I asked several people about the Church Health Center and they explained you are the good guys. I had to come and apologize in person."

The patient arrived later that day. It turned out he had come to us originally because of severe stomach pain, and we'd sent him to the hospital—the right thing to do. He was thirty-eight years old and had never been sick until that day. At the hospital he learned he had a hole in his intestine and had emergency surgery. A few weeks later he experienced pain in one arm, and it was then that the MS diagnosis emerged. A few weeks after that, he had a heart attack. Somehow he ended up seeing a neurosurgeon.

I could see why the young doctor, a resident in neurosurgery, was so determined to help. He truly had the patient's best interest at heart, but he was just a little too eager to fight. · · · · · · · · · · · · · · · · · ·

It seems to me that part of what that neurosurgeon was fighting against was the expectation that the "system" did not want to help the patient. I have no doubt that most doctors—and patients— could tell their own stories of trying to cut through medical and insurance bureaucracy.

And I think of people like George, whose hand was cold for nine years because the "system" let him down. All he wanted was to be able to work and to maintain some independence. Instead he became one of the vulnerable, with no one to invite him to sit in the empty chair, no one to truly listen to his story and walk alongside him to a solution with dignity.

COMMUNITY CARES

People get hemmed in by their own circumstances, and this leads to isolation that both robs us of our sense of dignity and leaves us needlessly isolated.

Tommy was a successful music professor at Tulane University in New Orleans. When he contracted HIV, it came out that he had been living two different lives for years. His family left him, and he lost his job. Suddenly he was all alone. By this point, recently out of seminary and after my ordination process had made the basics of my health status available to others, I had been sharing my story of HIV when I spoke or gave interviews. Tommy read an article about me and tracked me down. He had relocated to his mother's house to die, and to get to know me. Tommy believed this might be his last opportunity to believe that God could love someone like him.

We shared our journeys for the next couple of years. I watched as Tommy went from being antagonistic about faith, the church, and the world to finding hope through music. He got involved in the little church choir of the church I was pastoring. Pokey and I were young, but the congregation consisted of people in the age bracket of sixty-five to eighty—and Tommy. He ended up being the choir director for the only musical the church had presented in the last twenty years. Right after the musical, he got sick and passed away.

My grandmother used to sing "Jesus Loves Me" to me at bedtime. Tommy's grandmother did the same for him. When Tommy was in the hospital for the last time, I went to visit him. He was drifting in and out of lucidity and mumbling about whether he had missed his chance to know God's love. "Jesus Loves Me" is what came to my mind. We have a song inside us, and not only are we meant to sing it but to sing it with others. Our paths intersect with people who need to hear about hope and good news.

The Church Health Center lives at this intersection, meeting people every day whose hope can be stirred by being treated with dignity and love.

In 2006 I was invited to speak at the Global Initiative for HIV and AIDS, organized by Saddleback Church in California. I spoke in the first session between well-known pastor Rick Warren and his wife, Kay. The next day, while I was standing on the veranda at the Saddleback campus, I noticed a young African woman in traditional garb and an American man on a cell phone who looked like he just stepped out of *GQ*. Because I had spoken the day before, they both approached me to chat.

The woman was the daughter of a chieftain in a village in Rwanda. She was present at the conference to speak about the needs of her country because Saddleback had adopted the nation of Rwanda. Five thousand church members gave one week every year to travel to Rwanda for various forms of ministry. The gentleman, from a wealthy family, was an attorney for a committee of the House of Representatives that had been working on issues of HIV-AIDS.

Her village was ravaged by HIV-AIDS.

His good friend from college had died of AIDS.

Though on the surface the two of them had nothing in common, their faith had brought them together on this shared journey of responding to the AIDS crisis. Faith not only helps us deal with the struggle of our individual lives, but it also transforms those struggles into open doors that become opportunities to do things we never would have done otherwise. These two people would never meet in any other context on the planet, but they began to talk about how they could help each other in their journeys. As much as faith is a responder to need, it is also an initiator of remarkable opportunity to come to the table, where everyone has a place, to do God's work together.

> *Our God, we seek to find you in our lives. We come not alone but joined together. Without you we are missing what makes us whole and what brings us joy. We long for your healing touch to cure what ails us and live bathed in the love that comes only from you. Amen.*

8

"I KNOW HIM BY NAME"

No one should have to feel alone.

Here's Scott:

Katie is well into her seventies, and I've been taking care of her for more than twenty years, including the years she fussed at God about her husband's suffering and death.

One day Katie said to me, "Dr. Morris, you don't know this, but for all these years I have prayed for you several times a week. Sometimes I pray for you three times a day."

Just hearing that made me sit back in my chair.

Katie continued, "Last week I closed my eyes, and right in front of me was Jesus himself! I told him I was praying for you, and do you know what Jesus said to me?"

I was still taken aback by the fact that Katie sincerely prayed for me and the Church Health Center so often, but what she said next was astonishing.

"When I told Jesus I was praying for you," Katie said, "he said to me, 'I know him by name.'"

The thought of Jesus knowing me by name is powerful. Surely that is how we all want to be known by God, but to hear this from someone to whom I have tried to offer care over the years struck me as profound.

Jesus said, "He calls his own sheep *by name* and leads them out. When he has brought out all his own, he goes ahead of them, and the sheep follow him because they know his voice" (John 10:3–4).

Katie's encouragement made me want to live a life where Jesus knows me by name and I hear his voice.

I left Katie with refills on her routine medications and an order to check her blood levels. It seemed a weak exchange for the gift she had given me. ·

When Scott tells stories about his maternal grandfather, it's clear he behaved as if anything was possible. "He's the greatest wheeler-dealer I've ever known," Scott says.

Scott was about six when his grandfather bought an airplane, hitched it up to his Cadillac, and hauled it down I-75 right through the middle of Atlanta. Then he traded the airplane for an apartment building.

Anything is possible.

The wheeler-dealer was also a promoter of Live Atlanta Wrestling, so Scott had a ringside seat on Friday nights. His grandfather went to his grave believing it was all real. Chief Little Eagle put his hands in his trunks and then slapped his forehead. Suddenly he was bleeding.

"Granddaddy, no one touched him," Scott insisted.

But his grandfather didn't believe the little boy's suspicions. Anything was possible.

Granddaddy was one of the first recipients of a bypass operation, but he lived only a few days afterward. At the time of his death, he owned several duplexes, and Scott's mother inherited them. The income they provided paid for more than a decade of higher education. The money ran out almost to the day Scott finished medical school.

Anything was possible for Scott's grandfather, and I think Scott thinks big in the same way by serving people like Katie. In the field of health care, we see a lot of group numbers and statistics. We learn useful information from research where people in the studies are more likely to be identified by an impersonal number than to be known by name. We learn the statistics and success rates of various treatment protocols. This is all clinically valuable. Clearly I have benefited from the science of health care.

But it's not the same as knowing each other by name and having at least a tenuous grasp on the life story that goes with the name. We all help each other move farther along the journey to health and wholeness when we know each other by name. That's what a community is about. When we make it a point to know people as individuals, with complex stories, we reflect the same relationship of care and intimacy that we have with God, who knows us by name.

Names to Remember

Here are some of the people Scott meets every day.

I begin most weekday mornings at the Church Health Center's walk-in clinic, an urgent-care service for people who have nowhere to go when they get sick with common illnesses. One day a big, burly guy who worked as a janitor came in with his wife, who had been a caregiver for thirty years. Her job is to go and stay with people who are sick. Ten days earlier they realized she was the one who was ill. Something was not right. She could not do the things she normally did. They had no insurance, but she was not getting better, so they came to the walk-in clinic. I knew she'd either had a stroke or a brain tumor. When I said she would need an MRI, a look of panic crossed her husband's face. How could they afford that?

"Don't worry," I said. "And you don't have to do this alone."

The man started to cry. "Nobody has ever cared for us," he said. "We've spent thirty years caring for other people, but nobody has ever cared for us."

Tyrone moved to Memphis from Detroit. He was clearly intelligent when I met him. At sixty-three, he was renting a room in a retirement community. I never was sure how Tyrone got his money, but a few dollars came into his hands from time to time. And that was the problem. Tyrone said to me, "I can't control my impulses. I got twenty dollars last week, and I went and bought a bottle of Crown Royal. I didn't want to, but it just kept buzzing in my head."

I talked to him about Alcoholics Anonymous, getting involved at Church Health Wellness, and a weekly worship service St. John's has for people in recovery called The Way. I wanted him to know help was available. He responded by saying, "When these things happen, I exaggerate how terrible everything is. I feel so deep, and I can't seem to crawl out." When I offered to meet him at The Way, his face lit up. "Somehow you just gave me hope. I have been missing that."

Time will tell whether Tyrone makes needed changes for his own health, but his story reminds me of the powerful force of fear that calls to all of us from the deepness within us.

For years I have been the doctor for Mr. Kahn, who came to Memphis in 1988 from Syria. He began working in a convenience store, and then managed to get his immediate family to Memphis. I treated him for his diabetes and hypertension for years, and then one day he told me, "I am going home to Syria for a visit. Why don't you come with me?" He went on to tell me what a wonderful country Syria is. "It is not like the rest of the Middle East. It is very safe. Christian and Muslim live side by side and we all get along." I was not able to go, but from that point every time I saw him, we talked about Syria.

One year, when I went to Israel, he looked hurt when I answered his question, "Did you go to Syria?" by saying, "No, I went to Israel."

"Why did you not go to Syria?" he asked.

This was, of course, before the civil war in Syria broke out. As the war unfolded, I thought about him every time I heard news of the fighting on TV. Because of Mr. Kahn, the tragedy was more personal.

Then, one day, I saw him in the clinic. He was seeing one of the other doctors, but I stopped what I was doing and went up to him. "I am so sorry about what is happening in your country."

He had a grieved, pained look in his eyes. I assumed it was for the general chaos in the country he loved.

Then he said, "Today, eleven people in my family were killed. Why all of this killing? Why?"

What else could I do but reach out and take him in my arms? "I am so sorry."

He wiped his tears. "I cannot believe it."

The situation in Syria has only gotten worse since then.

• • • • • • It's not uncommon for me to see patients who don't speak English. The population of Memphis represents many nationalities, many of them immigrants. One Mexican family came in speaking almost no English. I was lucky that day. Someone was available to translate. My patient was an eight-year-old girl who smiled when I looked

117

at her. She had the obvious features of Down syndrome, and she was there because she had a cold. I could offer little to treat a cold, but I was worried whether Maria had been fully evaluated for the complications that can go with Down syndrome, such as heart defects. It turns out the family members all have green cards, which means she should qualify for Medicaid. Recently she had lost her coverage.

Speaking through the translator, I kept asking questions. The father had worked for seven years as a tree trimmer and, during that time, Maria qualified and had a pediatrician she went to. But about a year ago, he launched his own business. For some reason, Human Services asked for proof of his income, and they did not accept what he gave them. Therefore, Maria was cut off from Medicaid.

As we talked, the mother looked through her pocketbook and pulled out an expired Medicaid card. It was attached to a Catholic prayer card with a picture of Mary on it. I looked over at the child named Maria. I smiled at her again and she smiled back again. I called our social worker and asked her to work to get Maria back on Medicaid. Without our help, what was this family to do for this little girl?

· · · · · · · A forty-eight-year-old man who lives in a boardinghouse was very pleasant, but freely offered, "When you are living with ten to twelve other people in a house, coming and going at all hours, it's hard to get any rest." He recently had started a job, but had not worked long enough to have any benefits. For the last month, he had been feeling bad and had lost about fifteen pounds. Then he started vomiting and was not able to go to work.

When I examined his abdomen, he was tender. His skin was tinged with yellow. His white blood count was high, and so was his bilirubin, which accounted for his jaundice. My instinct told me this was pancreatic cancer, but I hoped I was wrong.

I told him I was worried he had a serious problem, and I was sure he knew but was hoping for the best.

"Doc, can you write out something I can send to my job? I can't lose this job."

"Sure," I said. "I will tell them you can't work right now." I doubted he would ever be able to work. "Are you okay with staying at the boardinghouse?"

"Sure. It's clean."

I said what I thought was the most important thing. "From now on, you don't have to face this alone. I promise you we will help you through it."

• • • • • • I saw a thirty-two-year-old man from Yemen who had a minor medical problem, but it was clear his stress level had made him a wreck. He was a U.S. citizen and worked at a convenience store in north Memphis.

He had been in the United States for twelve years and was married with four children, ages five to fourteen, who were all living in Yemen. He had been trying to bring them to Memphis for years.

Since Yemen has been closely tied to al-Qaida, scrutiny for any Yemeni immigrants is tight, and he understands the problem. Yet, as he points out, "My wife and I just want to be together. We didn't make it good or bad."

His visible anxiety was over their current struggles as a result of the unrest in Yemen. Living in a Muslim country, his wife is not allowed to go out in public alone. Yet in order to cook, she needs a propane tank. Her brother has been refilling the tank for the family, but he had been out of town for the last several days. My patient was worried whether his children were eating.

He explained to me that the family's visas were approved five years earlier, but that bureaucracy had prevented the final papers being signed. In 2008, all seemed set. Then at his wife's medical exam, the physician wrongly checked a box saying that she "chews khat," a narcotic substance common in the Middle East. This led to her visa being denied for three more years. That time had come and gone, and still nothing had happened. He had repeatedly contacted political leaders' offices to no avail.

As luck, or grace, would have it, my wife and I shared a meal with friends that evening. Our congressman was also at the dinner. The next day I called his office to get help with the visa. It took me five minutes to cut through the bureaucratic tape my patient had been dealing with for five years.

Ella was six years old and was suspended from school for two weeks for biting her teacher. She was repeating kindergarten, and her behavior threatened to hold her back again. Her mother is a receptionist with other daughters who are doing fine and have no conduct problems.

When I asked Ella if she knew why she was there to see me, she said, "I bit my teacher. Twice."

"Have you done anything wrong?"

"I got mad and tore up the toys and I glued the other children's papers together."

Ella clearly understood that what she had done was wrong and had a sense of remorse. But when I asked her, "Why did you do that?" she just looked at the ground.

Her mother was definitely at her wits' end. She had tried everything she knew to do, but to no avail.

"Have you seen the school psychologist?" I asked.

"No, they told me to come here."

The city schools have a legal obligation to evaluate children like Ella but, because there are so many problem children in the inner city, the waiting list can be long. The problem is worse because Ella was going to a charter school, and the city schools, despite their obligation to help, rarely reach out to children in charter schools or make the process easy.

I did not think Ella had ADHD, nor did I think she needed any medicine. She was angry at something, and her actions showed it. Thankfully, a psychiatric nurse who works with us was with me the whole time. She would be able to push the school psychologist to evaluate Ella and help make a plan.

Once again, I said the same thing I say many times, "From this point on, you do not have to feel you are alone in this problem. We will stick with you."

• • • • • • A pair of sisters, both in their fifties, came to see me. One had come from Mexico a few years ago and was working in a Mexican restaurant. The other had arrived recently. She had a chronic disease. Two years earlier, her husband, a bus driver, had died from a tragic lymphoma. She had several children and could not find a job to support them. I've learned this is a common reality in Mexico. If you are female and over fifty, it's almost impossible to find a job. After two years, she was desperate to provide for her children.

The sister living and working in Memphis went back to Mexico, where the two women pooled their money to come up with five thousand dollars to pay a coyote to smuggle them across the border at night with several children. As they made their way across the desert in the dark, the woman with an established life in Memphis fell and tore up her knee. Both sisters needed a doctor. The Church Health Center is now the medical home for both women and their children.

• • • • • • Reverend Pennypacker was an 83-year-old retired Episcopal priest who had been wanting to volunteer, but I had not yet sorted out how best to use him. Then one week he left me a voice mail saying,

"I cannot begin volunteering because I have had a recurrence of my cancer and will be having surgery."

The next week I called to see how he was doing. Mrs. Pennypacker answered and soon dissolved in tears. The operation had gone well from a technical perspective, but it changed her husband mentally. He believed he was on a cruise in the Mediterranean and was generally confused about everything. As I listened to her crying, I gave my opinion that he may have had a stroke, or it might be medication side effects. Obviously I couldn't be sure, and I barely knew them, but I wanted to say something of comfort. Though I had listened more than I spoke, she thanked me repeatedly for calling. It's amazing how it's possible to enter people's lives at critical points and not be aware how important you can be to them. · · · · · · ·

Care for the Spirit

"I know him by name," Katie heard Jesus say about Scott.

And at the Church Health Center, names matter.

Health—or lack of health—does not happen in a doctor's exam room. It doesn't come out of a prescription bottle. It happens in the context of real lives with real stories and challenges and disappointments and victories. So much of what brings people into doctors' offices happens in their spirits, or a clinical condition is complicated by what is happening in the spirit. Yet traditionally, at least in the modern era, we concern ourselves with the latest technologies to cure the body more than we concern ourselves with knowing names and hearing stories and coming alongside each other in understanding what it means to be healthy together.

"My patients simply refuse to do what I tell them to do."

Those are not Scott's words, but the reaction of another doctor to what physicians call "noncompliance." This label turns up in a medical chart if a patient does not follow through with something like instructions to take medication, get more exercise, do physical therapy, or make another appointment.

Too often what doctors really mean is, "You didn't do what I told you to do!" This approach is shaming, and it does not help people change their behavior.

Scott says, "My main job as a physician is to help people make changes in their behavior that lead to better health. Yes, I prescribe medicine, treat disease, and refer people to surgeons who seek to cure serious problems. For most people, though, I do the greatest good if I can help them live a healthier lifestyle."

Few people, even the very brightest, can fully remember everything the doctor says in the course of a visit. For that reason, at the Church Health Center, the staff works as a team in helping people with their health. While formulating the treatment plan is still largely in the doctors' hands, carrying it out is a team effort. The nurse, the dietician, the exercise specialist, the front-desk receptionist, the counselor—they all play vital parts in the process. When Scott promises, "You don't have to be alone anymore," he knows his team will be there to be sure he's speaking truth.

And he knows how transforming it can be simply not to feel alone, to feel that somebody knows your name and listens to your story.

"People rarely remember what you say to them, but they always remember how you made them feel." Though he says this a lot, Scott makes no claim that it's an original thought. But it's one that we should all be repeating.

Why do we believe there is greater virtue in doing things on our own? It's almost never true.

Where would the patients of the Church Health Center be if they turned away offers of help? Not healthier. Where would I be if I turned away offers of help? Not healthier. Where will our society be if we refuse to help one another? Not healthier.

Companionship on the journey toward health gives people tools, a plan, hope, a chance for control of their futures. And then they'll have the chance to come alongside someone else. If enough of us pay it forward, we'll see real change.

Together is a consistent image in the Bible, and we do well to embrace it in the way we share our lives and in the way faith draws us into an understanding of health.

Jesus sent his earliest followers into the towns and villages both to preach and to heal. And they went in pairs. One alone might cower and run, while two will hold each other up. Healing miracles point to the wholeness God desires for every person. We could argue that these pairs of disciples were the earliest health ministry partnerships.

God's desire for our well-being is still revealed in our journeys toward health and wholeness. We are not meant to be alone on our health journeys any more than God wants us to be alone in life.

COMMUNITY CARES

For the majority of my life, I've had a particular context because of my own narrative. I knew that my story helped to frame my approach to preaching, but I hadn't realized it also framed the way I approached ministry and serving in general. While not everyone has a story with the sorts of medically dramatic points mine has, nevertheless, their story frames the way they live out their faith. These framings can be very helpful, but they can also be limiting.

After I came to Memphis, I began to see that while my story and context were well received, they were also part of a bigger narrative. The main theme was not only about what God was doing in my life, but the experience of faithfully participating in the journeys of others, including people I did not agree with or about whom I understood little of the issues that were most important to them.

I learned two important lessons about learning to listen to stories and know people by name.

First, getting outside of my own frame of reference gave me experiences that sharpened the tools available to me for relating to and serving others. I had gotten used to people affirming my gifts in communication and discernment. Now I was beginning to better appreciate how using my gifts alongside the gifts of others would make us both stronger.

Second, while I had personal reasons to feel strongly about issues of addiction care, I had never been closely involved with this kind of work. I also had never been involved in combating the sex trade that exploits women and girls, and in Memphis I began to see this more closely. Both of these ministries—to people affected by addiction or sex exploitation—forced me out of my comfort zone.

For years I had taken for granted things I was doing and had a wheelhouse full of ways to explain how people should be involved in the things *I* cared about. Now I was listening better to issues that others cared about and seeing issues from perspectives other than my own. Getting out of my own context made me stronger in my own framework for service.

Congregations can experience this iron-sharpens-iron phenomenon when they intentionally seek to come alongside health ministries and embrace other opportunities to "know the names" of people they serve. Let me suggest three basic approaches to action.

First, broaden the nature of relationships in your life and community. This allows you to hear other perspectives not in an academic or programmatic way, but in a personal way. The only thing better than an idea is an idea that has a face to it.

Second, getting involved with other individuals will show you things you can do that you might never see if you remain insulated in your familiar surroundings and relationships. You may be surprised at how this brings focus to how you use the gifts you already have.

Third, stepping out to understand other perspectives and work alongside other gifts will go a long way toward building a coalition of support for meeting needs in the community. The more you get involved in areas not related to your original passions, the more you show people new doorways and new ways of thinking. At the same time that your conversations are broadened, you will be broadening the conversations that others have. Now the community is talking about getting something done.

No one should have to feel alone. Communities cannot reach their full potential if the various parts remain insulated. Insulation brings about a sedentary mindset, where parts of the congregation or community do things the same old way. And no matter how new and creative that way once was, it will cease to be effective. Fresh and continuous conversations will remind us of the names and faces of the people we serve.

> *God of all, help us to see the way you would have us go. When the time comes, may we all say, "I'm in. I'm in for the long haul. I'm in for the life of service and compassion you call us to live." Amen.*

9

LIGHT ON THE WAY

Hope doesn't happen all at once.

Here's Scott:

When Janis started coming to us in her late thirties, I treated her high blood pressure. Then I started seeing her five boys. I told our receptionist, Kim, that if we ever needed another person at the front desk we should hire Janis, and we did. She worked for us for fifteen years, and I taught all her boys to swim.

One day Janis was late to work. When she left her apartment to take her younger boys to school, they discovered a man had been shot and left for dead right outside her door. The whole family was traumatized, and I couldn't stand the thought of their staying in that building. I went to a local agency that builds homes for families who otherwise might never have the chance to live in their own houses and pleaded that the trauma and danger should put Janis's family at the top of the list. It worked. The boys are all grown, and Janis lived in that house for many years. ·

I've heard enough stories like this from Scott that it doesn't surprise me. Rising to the challenge is part of his personality. When Scott was eleven, he played in a local Little League championship game. Everybody knew the opposing team had the best pitcher in the league. Scott's turn at bat arrived, and his grandfather shouted for everyone to hear, "I'll give you five dollars if you hit a home run."

Scott hit that home run—only the second he'd ever hit. For him it was a life-changing experience of rising to the challenge.

Maybe you've seen the old cartoon that shows a man mopping a flooded floor. He is working hard, with sweat pouring off his brow as he fills his bucket with the water from his mop. Only if you look in the background of the illustration, over his shoulder, do you see a huge water spigot turned on full blast.

Scott saw this decades ago while listening to a medical missionary give a talk. The speaker's point was that without turning off the faucet, the problem will always be insurmountable.

"He was talking about an overseas setting, but I thought that could be Memphis," Scott says. "We had thirty-five thousand patients at the Church Health Center and might have one hundred thousand before I retired, but what were we doing to turn off the faucet?"

If we're really going to have a conversation about wellness in our society—and in our congregations—that's the essential question. Hope for a well, whole life of joy and love doesn't happen in one fell swoop. First we have to turn off the faucet. Then we have to clean up the mess.

Body and Spirit

When Scott goes to work in the morning at the Church Health Center's clinic, he never knows what awaits him, but he does know that many of the patients he sees carry burdens he can't treat medically. People come not only because their bodies fail them, but also because their lives are broken.

One otherwise healthy woman came in because she could barely hear, a condition that happened abruptly. She felt she could not perform her job safely if she could not hear, and wanted a note her employer would accept as reason to excuse her from work for a few days. Based on the frequency with which she asked Scott to repeat himself, it seemed evident that she was not hearing.

But why?

He looked in her ears and saw nothing amiss. As he talked with her, he learned that in addition to working all day, she was caring for her dying brother in her home at night. She was afraid he would need her and she would not hear him.

Fear manifests itself in our health and life whether we name it or not. This is only one story. From our joint experience with pastoral work and health care, Scott and I could tell you dozens—hundreds—that would illustrate the same point. People come to us broken in spirit, crumbling in their relationships, anxious about the future, desperate for a pastor or a doctor to fix things.

Give me a pill.

Say a prayer.

Send me to a specialist.

Tell me what to do.

Somehow, just make things better.

We both see people all the time who do not connect the dots between realities in their spirits and realities in their bodies. The truth is that our bodies and our spirits have a causal relationship that works both ways. What happens in our spirits—for good or for bad—shows up in our bodies, and what happens in our bodies shows up in our spirits. When something goes awry in one dimension, too many of us look for solutions—hope—only in that dimension.

Is it any wonder that we do not find the relief we seek?

Nobody lives in one dimension. And we all know what fear feels like.

Fear is powerful.

In the nineteenth century, Charles Darwin believed we had evolved our response to fear. To test his theory, he went to the zoo in London and stood before a highly poisonous snake to let it lunge at him. He wrote, "My will and reason were powerless against the imagination of a danger which had never been experienced." He had never been bitten by a snake, just as people who are afraid of flying have never been in a plane crash. It is the anticipation of dread that generates fear.

Scott sees fear every day. Here are a couple more of his stories about the way fear can suck hope out of us.

I saw a twenty-year-old woman who came from Mexico as a small child and grew up in Shelby County, but remains undocumented. She's had a long-term kidney problem. Whenever she had an event that required medical care, usually in the ER, she was always told to follow up with a nephrologist. But without access to insurance, seeing specialists was not a realistic option for her parents. Over the years, most of the time she did fairly well medically. Then she got sick and was admitted to the hospital in renal failure. After receiving dialysis, she was discharged on a Sunday. She came to us the following Wednesday needing dialysis again.

The last line on her hospital discharge instruction sheet said, "Return to home country for dialysis."

Was this even a realistic option for someone who left so long ago and had little memory of ever living in Mexico? And what was she supposed to do for dialysis in the meantime?

I ferreted out that her family had come from near Guadalajara. "Do you still have any relatives there?" I asked.

"Yes," she said.

"Will you go back to Mexico?"

She hesitated. "What will happen if I don't?"

"You'll die." I had no other answer to offer.

"I guess I'll go."

We were able to verify that a place in Guadalajara could provide dialysis, but their response was, "She's an American."

I can see their point. Her parents chose to come here. She had no say in the matter. She grew up here, went to school here. Now that she needs costly care at public expense, we want to shift the burden back to Mexico. Her life—literally—was caught in the immigration debate.

We found a place in Nashville and sent her there that afternoon for dialysis. I called Gary Shorb, who was then head of the Methodist hospital in Memphis, and he figured out a plan that would give her dialysis for a few months until she turned twenty-one.

After that? I didn't know. But she would die without dialysis. I knew that.

• • • • • • A jack-of-all-trades came to see me. A husband and father of two, he worked sixty hours a week and was the sole financial support of his household—and he was uninsured for medical care or disability. He had tried to pull a half-ton item with a chain and injured both his shoulders. Now he was in pain and could not lift his arms. His boss told him about the Church Health Center, and he came to see us. We had an orthopedist on site that day who gave an immediate opinion.

The man had destroyed his rotator cuffs.

With time, the pain would abate, but without surgery, he would never raise his arms normally again.

We could arrange his surgery and follow-up care, but the procedure would mean being heavily immobilized for three months and another three months for rehabilitation to full use.

His choice came down to never having full use of his arms again, or six months of no income at all for his family. He did not cry, but he came very close. I can only imagine the fear he felt in the face of this impossible no-good-option decision. Either choice meant risks, and either way he would have to live with the outcome for the rest of his life.

Now that is a fearful moment. •

A Handle on Hope

Turning off the faucet begins with giving people reason to hope. The Church Health Center makes no claim to be able to solve every problem its doctors see. It does, however, promise to come alongside people who face hard decisions or who are willing to make changes for better wellness.

After Scott heard the missionary speak about turning off the faucet, he attacked the question of what it would take to slow the gush of preventable diseases and behavioral health issues that bring people to doctors. One strategy was to incorporate preventive medicine and community health on a larger scale into the work of the Church Health Center. The Church Health Center had always offered a couple of treadmills for exercise and the services of pastoral counselors and social workers for crisis situations, but it was time to do this for the community, not just the patient base. In 2000, the Church Health Center opened Hope and Healing, an eighty-thousand-square-foot state-of-the-art wellness facility available to the entire Memphis community. "We emphasize meeting people where they are," Scott says, "and have been able to attract people to our programs who have never succeeded on their own in making behavioral changes."

The new center was called "Hope and Healing" because hope would open the doors to healing. By the time I arrived in Memphis over a decade later, the facility was officially known as "Church Health Wellness," but the original name often pops up in local parlance—perhaps because it captures exactly what people crave.

When the facility was less than a week away from opening, the staff worked feverishly to be ready on time. A newspaper reporter and photographer came to take photos and tour the building for a front-page story. It was easy for Scott to show them around and explain what the Church Health Center was planning to do. But one question stumped him. "Do you think it has turned out as well as you hoped?"

Scott laughed nervously and said, "It will either be the best thing I ever do or it will bring us down."

We are all broken in one way or another, but that does not prevent us from helping each other move toward a better sense of wholeness and health.

Preventive medicine is a term rising in popularity these days, but what is it? In reality, it usually consists of the doctor telling you to stop drinking, stop smoking, lose weight, and get more exercise. If we're honest, for most of us, it goes in one ear and out the other. And doctors know this. They see patients come in with the same issues in every visit and no indication that the patients have made any changes. Lack of information or instructions generally is not the issue. This approach is just not working.

Perhaps that's because the health care system is not set up for listening to what's broken in people's lives beyond what turns up in the lab work.

Perhaps it's because willpower is overrated when we try to make changes in isolation.

Perhaps it's because we're not meant to be bearing our burdens alone.

Perhaps it's because as communities we don't work hard enough at developing innovative solutions—even though we know the old answers are not working.

For instance, childhood obesity is a huge and growing health care challenge. We might think the obvious answer is for kids to get off screens and be more active. But what if they live in an area where it's not safe to be outside on their own? What if they're not good at sports or just plain don't like active games? What if their families can't afford the fees for organized programs? What if there's not even a park where the family could walk the dog together or throw a Frisbee? It's not enough to tell parents kids should be more active if we don't think creatively about what gets in the way of that goal.

Every day Church Health Wellness looks for ways to remove these obstacles. In an effort to address some of the root problems of children in the inner city, the Church Health Center has developed creative exercise programs, such as a partnership with Ballet Memphis to do creative movement with children who otherwise would be sedentary. Child care can be a challenge for parents who themselves would love to go to the gym. The Church Health Center offers a solution that not only is affordable but also engages children in activities that build healthy habits. Child Life Education and Movement is not the kind of child care that parks kids in front of a video while parents exercise. Rather, it's a program that supports even young children in healthy choices and living patterns.

At Church Health Wellness, health education includes classes, nutrition counseling, exercise plans, and group meetings. Wellness members receive an exercise assessment and an exercise plan at varying intensity levels. In addition to the usual exercise equipment and sports courts most gyms offer, Wellness has a heated therapeutic pool available to members for pain management and to maintain flexibility. Wellness education groups cover diabetes, arthritis, weight loss, stress, and smoking cessation. A health information resource room contains a variety of printed information but also high-speed Internet stations so members can access current health information. A state-of-the-art teaching kitchen with six cooking stations allows participants to interactively learn how to prepare healthier meals, including how to modify favorite recipes to improve their nutritional value without taking all the fun out of them.

I've seen this integrated approach make an enormous difference in the life of someone who attends my church. Marian was bipolar and lived with limited resources. As far back as she could remember, she heard advice that she needed to be involved in a fitness program. It would make her body stronger, improve her mind-set and self-esteem, and help her medication be more effective in regulating her moods. If you have resources, access to a fitness program is easy to obtain. But for someone like Marian, it was out of reach. In contrast, Church Health Wellness operates on a sliding scale, and it offers so much more than physical fitness coaching. Marian could find companionship and encouragement to understand the body-spirit connection that could make a difference for her. And it did.

Coming alongside people will make *preventive medicine* mean something. Creating a community has the power to change health.

Doris was a likable, attractive forty-six-year-old African American woman with dark, shining skin, a pleasant smile, and warm eyes. Yet she seemed so alone and defeated. It took Scott a while to figure out why she had come to see him. It came down to "I'm tired."

In a few days, she was going into a new drug treatment program—her seventh attempt to get clean of her addiction to crack.

When Scott saw her, she hadn't had any for a week, and she was feeling the immense sense of guilt people often have when they finally break from using it for a while.

"There is nothing you can tell me that I haven't heard before," she said. "I know I have to do it myself. I'll do anything to have my life back, but I've said that before. I've lost my job, I've lost my family, I've lost everything that was any good about my life."

Scott rolled his stool over to her and held her hand. After a minute he said, "Why don't you come to our exercise classes? Make it be like AA. You can exercise instead of smoking crack."

"That's a new one." She smiled. "It's worth a try."

Something Better

A daughter said to her father, "Dad, before you became a bishop, I cannot remember seeing you cry. Since you became a bishop, I cannot count the numbers of times I've seen you cry."

It's not an uncommon scenario. Clergy leaders almost always point to the church as the source of their stress—though they rarely say that the church offers any help—and stress takes a toll on their overall health.

In the denomination Scott and I share, United Methodist ministers are 20 percent heavier than the rest of the population. The stress of ministry leads to bad eating habits, lack of exercise, a dearth of emotional self-care, and cautious friendships. It's no different in other denominations. Scott observes, "Pastors are reluctant to go to the gym to exercise during the day because someone may chastise them for not being at work, but going in the evening is not possible on a regular basis because of the frequency of church meetings that accommodate everyone else's schedules. And few people are tuned in to the pastor's spiritual life because the pastor is supposed to have it all together."

He's right. I certainly experienced this phenomenon during my difficult season in Florida, where I dropped my guard about my own health.

The Church Health Center offers hope to leaders who may feel they have few options about where to turn. "Life of Leaders" is a three-day full-scale health evaluation. The participants have been bishops, district superintendents, national program staff, and local pastors from a variety of denominations.

The good news is that most leaders respond with enthusiasm to the support they find through Life of Leaders. Many have restructured their lives to make positive changes that address the dysfunction affecting their wellness. We can't have healthy congregations if we don't have healthy leaders. How can leaders offer hope that they don't experience for themselves? Giving faith leaders hope for their own health and wellness also enables them to help people in their congregations who crave the chance to exchange fear for hope.

A fifteen-year-old came to me and asked me to teach her how to do oral sex. She got it in her head—probably from her boyfriend—that this was not having sex but merely a way to please the boy. She couldn't see that he was pressuring her to do something she didn't want to do. Why did she ask her pastor, of all people, to help her with something like this? Had she completely separated the act from any moral meaning? Certainly it seemed that way. Or was this also her way of turning to someone she trusted to help find her way out of the waters rolling over her head?

At the center of hopelessness is fear that nothing else is possible. Fear is not a point in time, though it may begin there, but rather a lens through which we see the circumstances in which we find ourselves. Hopeless people do not make plans for the future. We make changes when we believe we have a chance for a changed future. Without that belief, what's the point? If a fifteen-year-old girl doesn't believe she deserves a future with a man who treats her with respect, why wouldn't she give in to her boyfriend's pressure? If a man doesn't see a future where he might have an income above the poverty line, why wouldn't he spend the money in his hand on immediate satisfaction? If a person with a chronic disease doesn't see a future of wellness and meaning, why even bother to take medications?

We all need to see something better in our futures—and have some sense of control in creating and sustaining that future. Hope is a central part of how we make our way in the world, but we do not attain hope alone. We help each other see the way out. We help each other see the wellness that lies ahead. Hope requires flesh! It doesn't have much meaning in the library. If we want to create lives of hope, cities of hope, we have to be in the business of hope together. This is what Church Health Wellness provides for so many people.

Hope for health care.

Hope for belonging.

Hope for connection.

Hope for love.

Hope for joy.

If we're going to turn off the faucet, we need to lean into the lever together.

While hope and fear pull in opposite directions, faith may be the bridge we seek. We may associate hope and faith, but fear also mingles with faith. We can want very much to believe one thing while at the same time fear that something else is more likely. The New Testament story about Peter walking on water comes to mind.

One night Jesus's followers begin a trip across the lake, expecting to row through calm waters, but they find themselves caught in one of these abrupt windy squalls. Fear strikes.

So Jesus, who was not with them, does what any sensible rabbi would do and walks out on the water to help. "Take heart, it is I; do not be afraid."

We would like to think the disciples then let out a collective breath of relief; but remember, fear is involuntary. They're not sure. Peter speaks for the bunch. "Lord, if it is you, command me to come to you on the water."

Jesus speaks again. "Come."

Peter gets out of the boat and walks on water toward Jesus. So far so good.

But the wind is still blowing, battering the boat and raising waves. Peter wants to believe he can walk on water, but he looks around and see the insecurity, the impossibility. The reality is that he *is* walking on water, but that is not what he sees. He sees the fear-filled threat rather than the faith-filled reality. And he starts to sink.

As Jesus reaches to pull Peter out of the waves, he says, "You of little faith."

It is not difficult to see ourselves in Peter. Jesus knows the frailty of our human condition—we of little faith. Yet he brings about the transformation that points us toward hope for healing in body and spirit.

Hope doesn't happen all at once, any more than handing someone an insurance card makes the person healthy. But that doesn't mean hope for wellness doesn't happen. A story of one of Scott's patients from years ago is a good reminder.

"Anna was a little girl whose mother brought her to us because she could not hear, and the family had limited resources to pursue medical treatment," Scott says. "She was ten years old at the time. We ended up arranging the first in a series of surgeries that led to restoring Anna's hearing. When I got an invitation to her college graduation I knew I held in my hand tangible evidence that our work made a difference, that it made lives better."

Hope changes lives. But hope doesn't happen in a vacuum. It happens in a community. It happens where faith is welcome. It happens where love abounds.

COMMUNITY CARES

My family does a mission trip to Mexico together every year. In the compound where we stay, there are two water faucets side by side. One releases water that has been filtered so it is safe to drink. The other is simply for washing up. It's important to keep those two faucets straight. Both are useful and needful, but mixing them up can be dangerous.

Fear and hope are like those two water faucets. The right kind of fear motivates a lot of good action, so the fear itself is not useless. Some sense of the repercussions of neglecting an action helps us to accomplish what needs to be done. For me, for instance, the fear of letting people down helps me get more done.

But I don't want to drink from that faucet.

A good dose of fear keeps us framed, but it's not what we want to swallow day after day. Hope doesn't happen all at once, but it is what nurtures us and restores us and transforms us. If we get hope and fear mixed up, it's dangerous to our well-being. Faith filters out fear and leaves us with hope that is safe to drink. In the same way that safe drinking water is fundamental to physical health, hope is fundamental to a whole, well society. Recognizing together that our lives have a spiritual dimension that contributes to overall health is a summons to help each other let our faith filter out what is toxic, both to individuals and communities, and fill our cups with hope that sheds light on our journeys.

God, who cares about every hair on our heads, every sparrow in the field, every blade of grain, help us to trust that your justice rules the day even when we are unsure what to think. May we be a place of refuge, a source of joy, and a light in the dark. Amen.

10

EYE
TO EYE

Look for the person who has created trust.

Here's a touching story from Scott about the intertwining
of trust and human dignity:

One of the first patients we ever saw at the Church Health Center
was an elderly woman from Thailand. She always came with her son,
who was devoted to her and constantly worried about her health.
For years I talked to her through her son while she sat and smiled at
me. One day when she came in, I knew something was wrong. She
had lost weight and appeared ill. It was necessary to examine her
thoroughly, so I asked her son to step outside. Merilyn, one of our
nurses, and I were left to communicate with her the best we could.

We maneuvered her to the examining table and motioned for her to step up. Nothing happened. Finally, it dawned on us that she was ready for us to *lift* her onto the table. And we did. She had complete trust in us to hold her up.

Eventually, and with great effort, I completed the exam and left Merilyn to help the patient dress. After allowing what I thought was plenty of time, I returned and opened the door to see the elderly woman completely naked with her arms around Merilyn, who lifted her carefully and lovingly off the table. The sight was a powerful image of compassion. And I felt the enormous responsibility of deserving the trust she placed in us. Both trust and compassion are difficult to define, but I know them when I see them, as I did that day in Room 5. •

No doubt Scott will never forget that patient or the lesson about frailty and trust that she taught him. I can see the impact of that day in Room 5 threaded through the Church Health Center all these years later. Scott won't let anyone forget.

I have my own story of trust that I will never forget.

I was sixteen.

My mother was keeping something from me, and I didn't know what. She did what parents so often do—get all the facts, understand the big picture, and seek the right moment for conversation. The difference was that this conversation had the potential to shred the future.

I knew from her face that something was wrong, but I had hemophilia, so hospital visits and tests and complications punctuated my childhood at regular intervals. I was in the hospital this time for eye surgery. My mother routinely had plenty of reason for concern, and I didn't think it was anything more than that.

My eye got better. I went to school and church in my small town in Mississippi. I made friends. I played golf. Ten months after that confusing look on my mother's face, the day came for my doctor to tell me what had put it there. When I had eye surgery, I tested positive for HIV.

The doctor now explained to me how they expected my physical condition to deteriorate because of the virus. He guessed that I had already been infected for several years as the result of a transfusion to treat my hemophilia before blood was routinely screened for HIV. The test at the time of my eye surgery only revealed what had silently lurked without symptoms.

I wanted to know how much longer I had to live.

Three or four years.

Was I not even going to get a chance to find out what life might be like as an adult? Had my future been shut down with one blood test? I hated the thought that my life could be over because of something out of my control.

I went home to my mother, stunned. What else could I feel in such a moment? Hemophilia is not an easy disease, but I had learned the necessary patterns of living and taking care of myself. HIV was a monster ten times as big. A hundred times. A thousand times.

And I was going to have to tell Pokey. The reason my mother finally decided I needed to know about the HIV was that she was afraid I would become intimate with Pokey without knowing the true danger in that decision.

I had a lot of trouble with trust after that. When somebody else makes a decision about your life, for good or for bad, that colors you. New questions skulk in every relationship or situation. Are you telling me everything? What are you keeping from me, even if you're not actually lying?

If trust can be so easily breached even among relationships rooted in love, imagine the scale of distrust possible in societal conversations about issues that affect us all, such as health and health care.

How jaded we can become about trust. Do we trust politicians to make the right decisions about health care laws? What about the Supreme Court? And insurance companies—will they ever be something other than entities we should expect the worst from? How can they possibly have our best interests at heart?

Everybody makes mistakes, even people with the best of intentions. Sometimes this reality is reinforced in ways we wish we did not have to admit. Here's one example from Scott:

"Scott, can I talk to you about this chart?" Tom White, one of our long-term retired volunteer physicians who reviewed charts, approached.

"Sure, Tom, what's up?"

"Well, you saw this chap last week for chest pain, which you didn't make much of. I'm afraid he went and had an MI on you."

Tom said it gently, but it struck like thunder. A myocardial infarction? "How do you know that?"

"I was reading his electrocardiograph and noticed a little ST segment elevation in the inferior leads and called to see how he was doing. His son answered the phone and told me that night, after you saw him, he had more pain and went to the hospital. He's in Baptist now. He's doing fine, but apparently he did have a small MI."

I grabbed the chart from Tom. The patient was seventy-four years old. My note on the ECG was clear about what I thought. I had written, "I do not think it is his heart." But when I looked at the ECG, I could see what Tom was talking about. The ST segment of an ECG is often raised when a person experiences blockages in the arteries to the heart. It was a subtle change but, in retrospect, it was clearly there. How had I missed it? Was my patient actually starting to have a heart attack while I was seeing him, and I didn't pick up on the signs? It is a sick feeling to know you have messed up on something so serious, especially when someone was trusting you to do what was best. ·

Everybody makes mistakes. That's the reason Dr. White was reviewing those charts for Scott in the first place. When I learned of my HIV, I believed my mother had made a mistake in keeping it from me. But she was still my mother, and I knew she loved me. If we move past broken trust at all, and toward better health and wellness, it will not be because we have blindly decided to place our trust in nameless strangers in a government office. It won't be because we are determined to come out on top, to be right, to be the winner of the health care wars. It won't be because we somehow beat the system.

It will be because we return to seeing each other as the frail human beings that we are.

Trust begins in daring to share our resources, to be good neighbors, to set an extra place, to call each other by name, and to learn helpful lessons—rather than become jaded—from the experience of doing these things.

Hurricane Katrina in 2005 was a natural disaster that brought lessons about trust to the center of Memphis. I was not in Memphis at that time, but Scott was. Here is what he remembers.

· · · · · · · I see the line every morning. And every time, it compels me forward.

The Church Health Center walk-in clinic opens at seven in the morning. I don't know what time people arrive to be sure they can be one of the first in line. They always are there before I am, lurking at the front door, listening for the turn of the lock, watching for the moment the door cracks open. They are sick, or they wouldn't come. And they don't have health insurance. Those are two facts I know about every patient I see.

But this morning on the brink of September was different. Patients not only huddled around the door or stood in clusters on the walkway, but the line, thick and swarming, also twisted well down the street. I entered the clinic through the rear door as I always do and donned my white coat. By now the doors were open. Striding down the back aisle and turning left, I peered into the waiting room—which looked more like an urban bus station after two days of canceled routes. People were everywhere—slouched in chairs, leaning against walls, sprawled on the floor. The smell of humanity clung to every breath I inhaled. While our clinic serves an uninsured population, most of them have jobs. Personal hygiene is not normally an issue. Now we faced a throng of people who had not bathed or changed clothes in several high-temperature days.

Hurricane Katrina, which caused massive destructive flooding when it hit land in New Orleans on August 29, 2005, struck Memphis a few days later in the form of a displaced population the size of a lot of American small towns. Overnight the line of people who needed to see a doctor, and had nowhere else to go, multiplied beyond imagination. No one predicted how many people leaving New Orleans would end up in Memphis. Driving out of New Orleans, on highways in gridlock, people came to a fork in the road. For most of them, the goal was simply to get out, so their ultimate destination was more a matter of position in the traffic jam than intentional choice. At the fork, drivers in the left lanes went to Houston, Texas. Those in the right lanes headed north toward Jackson, Mississippi. But Jackson isn't a large city, and hotel rooms filled up quickly, so people trekked north another four hours to Memphis. Eventually ten thousand displaced people arrived.

I'm used to walking into an exam room and meeting the person who needs to see a doctor, and perhaps one family member present for support. Now entire families crowded into the small rooms. Most of the time only one of them needed a doctor, but they were sticking together—and who could blame them? They left New Orleans with nothing more than they could put in their cars or carry on a bus if they were lucky enough to get a seat. They were in a strange city where most of them knew no one, haunted by the reality that the homes and jobs and neighborhoods and churches they left behind were under water. One family I met who didn't get out ahead of the storm spent forty-eight hours holding their baby on the roof, waiting for rescue. Of course they didn't want to separate from family members.

At first most of the reasons for seeking medical care were simple and predictable. Someone injured a back or turned an ankle in the rush to get out of New Orleans. Then came the people who left their homes without routine medicines to manage chronic diseases. They knew they needed blood pressure or cholesterol pills, or an insulin-dependent diabetic knew a crisis loomed without medication. Though the scale of the need was magnified, this was routine for us. We knew what to do to treat these conditions, and we did it.

And then came patients with less predictable issues, with less textbook answers. When I walked into an exam room and met an African American man in his mid-twenties, he was shaking. My first thought was that he had a fever, and mentally I starting going through the steps of determining the source and planning how to treat it. Then he spoke, and I heard the waver cracking his voice.

"Doc, you gotta help me," he said. "I haven't had any Lortabs in a couple of days, and I don't have a source here. I need your help."

Lortabs. Hydrocodone. "How much are you taking?" I asked.

"Three or four of the tens, four or five times a day."

I swallowed. This was at least 160 milligrams a day, a lot of narcotics. It was no mystery why he was in visible withdrawal.

I held his chart in my hand as I studied him. Meeting patients who are seeking narcotics is not new, but generally they are not so direct. Under normal circumstances, the request might open the door for a conversation about going into recovery, and we are glad to help people when they are ready to make that choice.

But refugees from Katrina? They didn't choose to leave New Orleans, to be stripped of their worldly goods, to have their income ripped away, to wonder if they would ever see their neighbors again. This young man wasn't choosing the path to recovery, and considering the immense stress he already faced, it was absurd to think this would be the moment he decided to abandon his drug habit. With the stroke of a pen, I had the ability to make one thing in his desperate life better for a few days. I didn't have to be holier-than-thou and say that on top of everything else he was suffering, he also had to go through acute physiological withdrawal.

It just didn't seem to me that Jesus would take a tough-luck approach.

My pen may have wavered the first couple of times, but soon it was crystal clear to me that the right thing was to write prescriptions that would keep people arriving in Memphis with addictions from going into sudden, unmanaged withdrawal. If I sent people away without anything, they were likely to resort to thieving to come up with the dealer's price, inflated by demand, which meant someone else would be a victim. I didn't give these patients what they were used to getting on the street, but I gave them something they could take for a few days and use to begin a weaning process if they chose to. I fully realize most of them used those days to get connected to a dealer in Memphis—I could have told them where to find one because I had dealt with local addicts often—but I don't regret responding to them with compassion rather than judgment.

As we sorted through the Katrina patients during those initial days, I realized many of them needed specialty and subspecialty care. Our clinic is a family practice, so we often refer people to other doctors, but the numbers were swelling even in those first few days.

I picked up the phone, something I don't ever hesitate to do. With one call to the executive director of the Memphis Medical Society, I had him on board. He sent out emails and faxes to every medical practice in Memphis and got essentially universal support. The response was, "If you are from New Orleans, we will see you for free. Come." In less than forty-eight hours we had a wide-open door for Katrina patients and a system for funneling them to the finest care. By now I was certain the refugees would keep coming. At the time, no one knew it would be months before they could go home—if ever—but when they had health issues, the medical community was prepared to take care of them. I started to breathe a little easier.

And then someone said to me, "Have you been down to the Red Cross?"

The Red Cross was two blocks away from us. I'd had my hands full and it hadn't occurred to me to go down there.

"No," I said. "What's going on?"

"You need to see for yourself."

So I went.

It was like a scene out of *Gone with the Wind*. Picture Rhett and Scarlett walking through the streets after the Battle of Atlanta. People were laid out everywhere. Lines stretched for blocks, though it wasn't at all clear to me what people were waiting for. Exhaustion swirled like a mist in every slumped posture, every stunned set of eyes, every scrunched face craving a moment of shade from the early-September heat, every glance of dismay that the line didn't seem to be getting any shorter.

As people crossed the state line from Mississippi into Shelby County, they were directed to the Red Cross to receive vouchers for places to stay, food, clothing, whatever they needed. That's why they waited in interminable outdoor lines on a blistering day. I managed to wend my way into a basement room set aside for medical work, where I saw a patient with his head supported on a stack of books, an unusual piece of medical equipment to be sure. Someone with an otoscope squinted into his ear.

"I'm Dr. Morris," I said, "from the Church Health Center."

The guy with the scope gave his name.

"Are you a doctor?" I asked, puzzled at what he was doing.

"No. But I went on a mission trip five years ago, and they taught me to look in people's ears."

Indignation pulsed into my neck. "Wouldn't we do better to get this patient to a real doctor two blocks away?"

He didn't seem interested in my opinion or the service I offered. A few more inquiries revealed that if people left to seek medical care elsewhere, they would lose their places in line for the nonmedical services the Red Cross offered. They had nothing. They couldn't risk starting all over again for shelter and food. In the meantime, people with diabetes were becoming ill, and dehydration grew into a visible issue as people baked in the sun.

The not-a-doctor with the otoscope was not the problem. I marched off to look for the person in charge at the Red Cross with the righteous indignation of a fiery prophet.

"Is this really what Memphis has to offer?" I glared. "People with no medical training are treating people when we have created a system for the established medical community to take care of them."

You would have thought I had threatened to abduct her grandchild.

Essentially she told me where I could stick it. She had zero interest in our helping with a situation that looked like a war-torn developing country. *They* were the Red Cross.

"You are not going to do this," I said. "This is not okay. We have to find a way that people with real health issues are seen by medical professionals."

"We'll get back to you."

I was dismissed. And I didn't hear from them again during the crisis days. She didn't trust me, and I didn't trust her. I've avoided the Red Cross for years now, not so much because of their choices but because of my own on that day. Righteous indignation is just that—righteous. We *did* need a better plan. But I didn't win any friends by slamming a hammer around in a crisis, and after nearly twenty years serving the underserved in Memphis, I should have known better.

The chaos that cloaked Memphis went on for another ten days, and I kept doing the next thing that needed doing. Medications came to the forefront. Our clinic has always made sure that patients who need common medications get them at a price they can afford, but we didn't have stock on hand for the urgent overwhelming demand.

So once again I picked up the telephone. I called every major pharmaceutical company in the United States and asked for donations.

"I've read the papers," I said again and again. "I know you're being generous. I saw that you're sending drugs to Houston. But what about Memphis?"

Getting to the right person who could make the decision sometimes took fortitude, and I spent hours on the phone, but virtually every company named a drug and said, "Can you handle ten pallets?"

The truth was, I didn't have a clue what a pallet was. I just knew they had pallets to send and we wanted them.

Then the trucks started pulling up to our clinic, and the drivers came inside and said to the receptionist, "Where do you want me to put these pallets?" I doubt the receptionist knew what a pallet looked like either. Pallets came ten or twenty at a time via FedEx or UPS. Everyone's eyes widened at the sheer volume.

I only had to look at one pallet to get a pretty good idea of what I had gotten us into.

One pallet is a lot of pills. Ten pallets, or twenty, multiplied by the number of companies sending donations, was the highest-level mathematics I've ever had to deal with.

Volunteers came out of the woodwork to handle an enormous volume of drugs. Employees got their family members involved in sorting and organizing at Church Health Wellness, the only place we had the space necessary for the task. The donations were a combination of samples, packaged in small quantities, and stock bottles, which typically contain five hundred pills. Most people needed thirty. It was time-consuming to design a system that efficiently received donations, organized them, repackaged them, and got them out the door to the people who needed them in appropriate quantities. I was on the phone forever, but generosity at every level was impressive.

No one in Memphis could ignore the way circumstances stretched our city's resources like an overstuffed, distended trash bag on the verge of bursting. Fast food places and inexpensive restaurants around the city were packed. You couldn't just walk in and leisurely order a hamburger or a plate of spaghetti. Ten thousand extra people had nowhere to go. Just like what happened in Jackson, Mississippi, hotel rooms filled up. Katrina survivors wandered for weeks on end, never sure where they were going to be the next day—and looking for a cool place to escape the sweltering heat.

The longer this went on, the more we saw the next wave of repercussions of the hurricane. Travelers originally stressed by the urgency of getting out of New Orleans to save their own lives watched the nonstop news broadcasts and realized they had nothing to go home to. Many of them came from the Ninth Ward, which took the worst of the hit in New Orleans. Even middle-class or upper-middle-class people had no jobs or homes to go back to. As the shock of living in a catastrophe movie turned into real life, we started to see profound depression, anxiety, and true post-traumatic stress syndrome.

A counseling base has always been part of our health work, but these problems would strain anybody's capacity to deal with them. We had a limited number of psychiatrists, and medications were not going to solve these issues. People left our offices in tears over the fact that we could not fix their lives.

Churches wanted to help. They really did. My own congregation took on an entire extended family, put them up at a local retreat center, and provided everything they needed. This turned out not to be such a great idea. It was a sweet deal for the family, and they found reasons to stretch out their stay for three or four months, well after the acute situation subsided. While they were there, they trashed the retreat center, and it cost the church thousands of dollars to repair the damage.

Stories like this happened all around the city. Churches took in people with the best intentions to help in a crisis. What no one factored in was that many of the refugees had their own ways of surviving in dysfunctional situations in New Orleans, and providing what seemed like an open-ended free ride was not, ultimately, in the best interest of the people churches tried to help. Congregations opened their doors for people to sleep inside their facilities, for instance, assuming it was a temporary arrangement until people could get a grip on what happened and begin to make plans for what they would do next. The plans did not always emerge, however. Churches were sucked into a paternalistic role they never meant to play. Again and again, this created bitterness on both sides. Churches finally said, "You have to leave," and heard the stinging retort, "I thought you said you were Christians!"

The Red Cross may have been ineffective in dealing with the medical needs, but people of faith had lessons to learn as well. We all wanted to think the best about people in the emergency situation. The deeper truth, though, is that most of the people who got flooded out and lost everything were a reflection of the seedy side of New Orleans. Tourists like to party at Mardi Gras for a few days out of the year, and we romanticize the musical heritage of the city or places like Bourbon Street or the French Quarter. We see the parts we want to see. We have to remember that New Orleans consistently makes the top-ten list of poorest cities in America.

I recognize these people. I see them every day in my medical practice. Memphis is on the same list of poorest cities in America.

Twenty-five years ago I might not have reached so easily for my prescription pad because a young man was honest with me about his dependence on narcotics. My years in Memphis have shaped my understanding of what it means to help. Now, in the years since Katrina, when I talk about why I wrote those prescriptions, I see the startled flicker in people's eyes—and I take advantage of it. That's my opportunity to illustrate the moral challenges that come with the choice to help people.

It gets complicated.

I didn't come to Memphis because of hurricane flooding. A current of idealism led me here, and I wanted to make a real difference in health care for the poor and the quality of people's lives.

But I had a lot to learn about getting the job done.

I don't know what happened to the young man who needed narcotics. I do know that ultimately, if he is going to find health and wellness, he won't do it on his own. There is no "doctor-god" who can fix everything with a pill. Community, not the person with power to dispense pills, is what creates healing. While Memphis rallied with an outpouring of compassion for the droves arriving from New Orleans, the experience highlighted how fragile trust can be just when we need it most. ·

Does this story teach us that we should withhold trust because some people might abuse it?

I don't think so.

Anne Frank wrote, "How wonderful it is that nobody need wait a single moment before starting to improve the world." Every American schoolchild—and I'm sure many around the world—learns Anne Frank's story. If anyone had reason to view the world with pessimism, she did. Yet her diary is full of statements like this one and of belief that humans could do better for each other than the way she was treated as a young teenager who lost her life in a concentration camp. Everybody has the possibility to do something. That is Anne's point.

Scott often says, "Look for the person who has created trust. Often it is absolutely *not* the doctor." So who might it be? What role does trust play in better health in our society? And how can we actively be building trust that will serve us well in pursuit of better health?

Building Trust to Be an Agent of Change

T. O'Neal Crivens came to the Church Health Center board in the early days as the pastor of an African American church and took on the self-proclaimed role to "keep the Church Health Center churchy." He introduced Scott to a string of small churches, and Scott learned a lesson about common ground he might never have learned another way.

A lot of white people are aware of a few pastors of a few large African American churches and think that is where the influence lies. It certainly tends to be that way in the predominantly white megachurch culture, where we are impressed by size. But that's not true in the African American community. Even pastors of small churches receive considerable respect and are sought out as influential because of their roles. O'Neal insisted Scott needed to meet a slew of pastors of small churches and be willing to preach in their congregations as a step toward establishing his own credibility.

Even though he grew up in the South, Scott had little experience with African American church services. He soon learned that two or three hours was not an unusual length. None of this get-home-in-time-to-take-the-roast-out-at-noon business.

"At first, I would arrive at the time the service began and stay until the end," Scott says, "but I got to the point where I intentionally went an hour late. Someone escorted me to the front and I still sat there for a long time before the pastor introduced me. Then I got up to give my twenty-minute white-guy sermon."

One day a pastor leaned in just before Scott began to preach and said, "I forgot to tell you. We're on the radio and you have an hour."

That was an extemporaneous experience Scott will never forget!

But O'Neal's strategy proved to be right on target. Even preaching in small congregations yielded a widening network of trust. People became more aware of the Church Health Center and more likely to seek care there if they became sick and didn't have insurance. Getting into the churches also opened doors for building on another level of trust.

"During medical school I spent a summer in Zimbabwe," Scott says. "I saw up close the effectiveness of village health workers. A woman who already has the trust of the village might go through a simple training process on basic health issues. Then she becomes the eyes and ears of a professional health care provider serving that area. The village health worker, rather than a doctor or even a nurse, is often the first to identify when someone needs care—and she'll know how to make sure it happens."

The Church Health Center offers a similar model, which reaches into the congregations of Memphis with a congregational health promoter ministry. Health ministry in a congregation does not require medical professionals to be members. Most congregations have someone—usually a woman—who has already gained the trust of the congregation because of their previous experiences with her. People are already going to her for advice. The Church Health Center offers an eight-week training program on basic topics. The training covers community resources people may not be aware of, including nutrition; mental and emotional health; common health issues such as hypertension, diabetes, and understanding medications; and prenatal, well-baby, and women's issues. The course also takes on sexually transmitted infections, usually a taboo topic in the church even though these diseases happen to people there. After the training, the congregational health promoters become the eyes and ears of health care in the congregation. Like the women in the African villages, congregational health promoters may be the first ones to spot an unmet need and help people access the care they need.

Trust is at the heart of a system that helps people live healthier lives without being connected to politics or insurance cards.

Congregations are an asset more and more communities want to leverage for better health outcomes. Compassion, relationship, and training are a simple prescription that can make an enormous difference.

The Church Health Center has been building trust in Memphis for nearly three decades. That's commitment. They did not come in, throw money at something, find out it doesn't work, and close down. They are still there, growing, leading, and becoming of interest at a national level. Building trust—rather than assuming it—is changing health care.

Scott has always said, "Let's get to thirty years and then we'll know if we've got a good start on making a difference." He's just about there, and no one doubts that the Church Health Center is making a difference.

When I see the creative approaches the Church Health Center uses to improve health and wellness, in contrast to the questionable outcomes of many bureaucracy-heavy programs, I can't help pondering what we need to be able to trust each other for in these larger conversations. Transparency? Information? Partnership? Equality? Care? And what role do people of faith play in the process?

In the handful of years I've been in Memphis, it's clear to me that Scott is one of the most trusted people in town. Even people who don't know him directly are inclined to trust him because he has developed so many relationships that go out ahead of him. And in the process, trust becomes an agent of change for the health of the city.

Look for the person who has created trust.

COMMUNITY CARES

Finding out about my HIV status was a shock, and the circumstances affected my ability to trust for a long time. I was an adolescent whose world was shaken up. Why should I trust anyone? I still sometimes feel that familiar pang of suspicion, but over time I've grown to reflect on the topic of trust differently.

Issues of trust don't happen in a vacuum. They are always related to the broader picture of the relationship. Whether in the family or in the community, we cannot talk meaningfully about trust without also talking about relationship.

That said, it's always best to approach a situation as though someone is telling the truth, particularly if we don't have a relationship with trust built into it that might have been broken. Always give people the benefit of the doubt until they give you a reason not to. Benefit of the doubt is not the same thing as trust, but it is a naturally trust-producing agent, so it serves a purpose that is larger than what may be happening in a given moment.

Does that mean we should be naïve? I don't think so. Ultimately trust is earned, and the time frame is not always predictable. Building trust in a community happens over time—perhaps a *long* time. But in the context of relationship, even on a community scale, trust means that we are prepared for the other party to be proactive in sustaining the relationship and making beneficial decisions. This requires that we are also willing to do our part in sustaining the relationship and making beneficial decisions. In personal relationships and families, we experience a degree of intimacy and intensity that allows trust to build at a steady rate. Of course there are surprises, but the strength of the relationship makes room for listening, understanding, and forgiveness.

Congregations, neighborhoods, and cities will experience trust building more at arm's length because we don't always have the context of close relationship. This takes longer. One of the things communities often lack is the patience to allow trust to develop at a rate that can be the real deal, rather than turn our eyes to the next leader or program that promises a quick fix. It's easier to withdraw from the process or to move on to another setting than to see the longer vision of what trust can do.

Faith communities have a natural asset in that the people who are part of them share belief and purpose. The way the congregation functions is as a network of relationships of varying size and intimacy. People in churches are no closer to perfection than anyone else, but they do have the opportunity to choose to make relationships less distant. This builds the context for trust and strengthens the congregation to be a trust-producing agent in the larger community.

It all starts with looking at the nature of our experience with trust on a personal level. There may be some work to be done, as there was for me. From there we can see how trust has the power to change us, and through us to transform our communities.

Our God, we seek to experience the kingdom here and now. Come and show us your way. May love, not hatred, rule the day, and may your will be done. Amen.

11

OLLIE'S POUND CAKES

The person with the power
has the responsibility to be kind.

Here's Scott:

When Ollie was eight years old, she was the second eldest of eight children. And she watched her daddy beat and kill her mother, nine months pregnant, in the kitchen. She still doesn't know why. As she sees it, this was during the days of Jim Crow, so nobody cared about domestic violence in rural Mississippi. Her father was never prosecuted. Soon after, her older sister died, which left Ollie in charge of raising her siblings, even though she was only ten at the time.

A few years later, her father married a woman who saw Ollie as a rival and arranged for Ollie to be sent to her aunt's home in

161

Miami, Florida, when she was fourteen. She finished high school there, but while still a teenager got pregnant and had two children whose father didn't stay around. When Ollie's father became ill, her stepmother left town, and the family turned to Ollie to take care of her dying—yet still abusive—father. To support herself and her children, Ollie went to work as a maid for a physician.

Years earlier, Ollie's mother had taught her to make a pound cake. It wasn't hard, and Ollie developed a knack for it. People liked them, so now whenever anyone did something nice for her, she would make a pound cake as a way of saying thank you.

Ollie was twenty-eight when she married R. C., who worked at an antique furniture store. R. C. developed a gambling addiction and spent every penny Ollie earned. When she couldn't take it anymore, she divorced him. But six months later, when he had a new job reupholstering furniture, they remarried. Despite promises to change, R. C. returned to his old ways and Ollie divorced him again the next year. Around that time she began working for a man who owned a restaurant and who bought her an old Chevrolet. She says, "I didn't have anything to give him to thank him, so I started making ten or twelve cakes a year for him."

Ollie married and divorced R. C. for a third time, but when he developed prostate cancer, she let him move back in. Her friends told her, "I wouldn't take that man back." But she did, and she cared for him until his death. Two weeks before he died, he told her he had been having sexual relationships with two of her sisters for many years. Ollie was devastated and was never able to talk with her sisters again.

Ollie became a patient of the Church Health Center and would bring not one but two pound cakes to every visit. Usually, I'd eat a piece and put the rest out for the staff. Everyone knew when Ollie had been to the clinic.

One Thanksgiving, Ollie brought me two cakes even though she didn't have an appointment. She told me, "You are the only family I have that loves me."

I couldn't let go of that comment. I didn't know what I'd done that Ollie would see me as family, or how she sees my caring for her medical needs as love. But the fact is that I thought I did love her, if it is possible to love someone whom I have only seen while being her doctor. And one day I saw her on the calendar, but she didn't bring any pound cakes. She had cancer and struggled mightily. I took to calling her myself with the results of her many tests, even if it was a minor test and everything was normal. Normally I wouldn't do that, but somehow it seemed like the right thing for Ollie.

When she knew the end of her life was close, Ollie told me, "I don't own much, but I'm leaving everything I have to the Church Health Center. I need you, Dr. Morris. Will you take care of my dog?"

Ollie reminds me why I came to Memphis and why I stay. She had a complicated, traumatic life, yet she looked for hope, gratitude, and love. Health in the life of an individual—or a community—is so much more than normal or abnormal test results. · · · · · · · · · · · · · · · · · · ·

The year I worked in Pokey's family church alongside Reverend Walley was also the first year that blood tests showed initial signs that HIV was taking a toll on my immune system. The hematologist who had treated my hemophilia for years was still following my condition, and now he suggested I see an infectious disease specialist.

The doctors I'd known all my life were caring people who connected with me personally. No one blamed me for having hemophilia. No one worried that they would somehow catch the disease—which is genetic—by treating me. They wanted to do whatever they could to support my health and help me live as normally as possible. I was in love, going to college, and engaged in work I found rewarding. Though I was aware my health could quickly turn fragile, I did not have a dismal outlook.

All of this left me unprepared for my first experience with an infectious disease specialist who treated HIV-AIDS. The difference was not in the medical specialty, but in the reaction to the particular disease. After an exam, the doctor prescribed AZT, the antiviral drug that reduces the ability of HIV to replicate itself. Beyond that, he said they would treat specific symptoms as they arose, but that since I had already had the disease for a number of years, my health was likely to decline sharply before long and he could not do much about it. Then he left the room.

That was it? It was a good thing I knew how much I mattered to people who loved me and to God, because I did not matter to that physician. I did not go back to him, but this experience was a revelation of the fear and hostility that people felt about HIV, even people in the medical professions. That clinic was in the basement of the hospital, and HIV-AIDS patients had to use a separate entrance. The doctors who worked there were primarily studying the science of the disease, not caring for the whole person.

It was as if I had been slapped in the face to wake me up to what this disease really meant. I learned not to take kindness for granted.

Here's a story from Scott about one of his early encounters with AIDS:

· · · · · · · · When the Church Health Center first began, I was reluctant to tell people that we saw people with AIDS. I'm not sure what I was afraid of. I think I was worried that some patients might not come because of the stigma and uncertainty about the spread of the disease in 1987. I also know that I was at first very anxious myself about the disease. Despite my intellectual understanding, my visceral response was noticeable when I saw my first few AIDS patients. I clearly remember the first one. He came with a simple complaint, but quickly announced he had AIDS. Suddenly the room seemed much smaller. My heart was beating faster and my hands were sweating. I was not exactly afraid, but I was definitely uncomfortable.

All that changed a couple of months later when I met Thomas. He was the yardman for one of our volunteer physicians. He came because of an infection around his eye, but I already knew he was gay, so I suspected the infection might be related to HIV. The test came back positive, and it was my job to tell him. He took it better than anyone else I have had to tell such terrible news. But he was taking it *too* well. Every time I saw him, I began to think something was wrong. One day I sat him down, looked him in the eye, and asked, "Do you understand what your problem is?"

He looked back at me and said, "I understand what my problem is, and I know that God loves me."

Thomas taught me once again that God loves all of God's children, and Jesus reached out to those who were outcast. If we want to find Jesus, we may need to look for him among people like Thomas. · · · · · · · ·

While Scott admitted being nervous about how treating patients with HIV-AIDS might affect the Church Health Center, the lesson I hear in this story is his willingness to look deeper. He didn't stop with doing his job clinically. He wanted to know about the well-being of the patient as a person.

And he was willing to learn a simple but enduring lesson from Thomas, letting love rise above fear.

One of Scott's favorite expressions is "The person with the power has the responsibility to be kind." He tries to live by that maxim and surround himself with people who understand the necessity. Take Mike Bruns, one of the people who was chair of the Church Health Center. When Mike entered the building, Scott knew he still had at least fifteen minutes before Mike would arrive at his office. Mike would stop at every workstation on the way up and find out how people were. As the owner of a large, successful trucking company, he used to carry hundred-dollar bills and give them out for no reason. But Mike didn't always have this status. He first arrived in Memphis, with a wife and new baby, to work for a company that folded a week after Mike got there. His family could have moved back to Chicago, but instead Mike decided to create his own trucking company. While his wife worked behind the counter at Wendy's to put food on the table, Mike managed to buy one truck. Then he needed a load. Then he needed a driver. This was the beginning of Comtrak, now one of America's largest trucking companies. Mike believed that life is about creating memories, and he loved the Church Health Center because he connected with the working people it serves even decades after his own financial success.

At a restaurant in California, Scott once met another man named Mike who explained his personal philosophy of "counterbalance." He said he'd made it up, and so far it was working for him. Every time he did something he knew was wrong, either for his health or toward another person, he sought to restore the balance by doing two positive actions. If he got angry at a waiter, for instance, the next time he ate out he would overtip the waiter plus go out of his way to clean up the mess on the table. Mike figured that by maintaining a ratio of two to one, he would spend more time with healthy and helpful—and kind—behaviors. We could all learn a lesson from Mike.

Standing in the Gap

The U.S. health care system is full of gaps—gaps in access, gaps in care, gaps in outcomes, and gaps in kindness. If we were to close the gap in kindness in the way we think about health and health care, perhaps we would be more likely to close the other gaps as well. And we're fooling ourselves if we think that one piece of legislation, like the Affordable Care Act, will eliminate gaps and even the playing field when it comes to health and health care. Even the rosiest projections for health care reform leave twenty-three million citizens uninsured and do not address the question of undocumented residents at all. Let's face it: health care is full of power struggles around issues of accessibility and funding and even patients.

Where is kindness in the conversation?

The person with the power has the responsibility to be kind.

Nobody is perfect. Here's an experience that happened to Scott early on:

Some days I can't understand why I get the way I do. I have in mind that I want to be calm and serene. I want to be gentle and kind, but sometimes small and trivial things happen that cause me to feel frustration or anger, at times even rage. It's a terrible feeling. After it happens, I long to be done with it, but I cannot just throw it off. Worst of all, I sometimes fall into the terrible pit of lashing out at someone who is powerless.

A pharmacist called me once about a prescription one of the other doctors had written. It just so happened that the call came right after I had become frustrated over a small matter. The prescription in question was an unusual combination of drugs, but a well-accepted usage. The pharmacist did not understand the reason for the combination of medicines and smugly gave me a wrong-headed explanation of why she thought this should not be done.

I'm sure there was a gentle way of resolving the confusion, but I did not take that way. I gave the pharmacist a short lecture on the pharmacology of the drugs and the current practice of using these drugs together. I had a strong urge to assert my power. I was right with my facts, but I was wrong with my heart. And it did not make me feel better. I wanted to take it all back immediately.

Too often the more power people have, the more they abuse it. I'm sure this is why Jesus went to the poor and the outcast, whose hearts were open to the love of God. When I find myself caught in the web of power, I feel more distant from God. It's a terrible lesson to have to keep learning. God does not long for us to be more powerful but to be more humble. ·

The Church Health Center stands in the kindness gap in many ways, not the least of which is the demeanor of physicians and other staff who care for patients. But they also stand in the kindness gap by acknowledging the other gaps and moving as the gaps move. The Affordable Care Act is closing some of the gaps in health care, but even this sweeping legislation leaves people on the margins, uninsured. Also, being enrolled in a plan does not necessarily address affordability of out-of-pocket costs and deductibles or transportation to locations where needed care is available. It certainly does not guarantee that enough doctors will accept expanded Medicaid or subsidized plans to serve the increased numbers of people going on these rolls.

Not only does the Church Health Center expect to be open for a long time practicing poverty medicine and helping underserved groups of people access quality levels of care, but they also expect to continue to help younger doctors in particular see the need for standing in this gap.

A six-week course called "Serving the Underserved" creates space for productive dialogue on the topic of how poverty shapes health. Seventy-five medical students attend six sessions with featured speakers who are involved on a daily basis with serving low-income populations and seeing firsthand the ways in which being poor results in poorer health outcomes.

Scott and other senior staff from the Church Health Center, along with community leaders, present their perspectives on the effects of personal connection with patients in underserved populations. Students study the societal risk conditions that contribute to health care issues—the "social determinants of health." It's an eye-opening topic for many students to discover the complexity of poverty and the implications for health that possessing an insurance card will never address. An adolescent gynecologist talks about getting burned out in a specialty that should not even have to exist. Health professionals who practice both locally and abroad share their experiences of health care in poverty settings.

All the medical students get is a certificate from the Church Health Center; they get no academic credit, and they sacrifice evenings they could be spending cramming for the med school classes.

The Affordable Care Act says nothing about undocumented workers, but if we need a reminder of the broken humanity we share with all people, not just citizens, their stories cut deep. Here's one from Scott:

· · · · · · Two Mexican men were in the same exam room, sharing an interpreter. One was eighteen and the other thirty-five. The interpreter had been a patient for a long time. The younger man had a cough and a sprained ankle. As I always do with immigrants, I asked, "How long have you been in Memphis?"

"Two days."

"Where were you before?"

"Mexico."

He had just crossed the border two days earlier.

"Where did you cross?" I asked.

"Laredo."

"How much did you pay a coyote?"

"$3,100."

He was forthright with his answers.

At this point the interpreter broke in. "He's my nephew. His mother saved up the money for him to come to me."

He was worried about his cough because someone else on the crossing had been very sick. They were worried he might have tuberculosis, and I did a TB test.

The other man appeared in pain.

"He is my brother," the interpreter said.

His lower leg was red, swollen, and tender. I was worried he might have a compartment syndrome, which would require surgery. I took an x-ray, and fortunately one of our retired orthopedists was on hand to examine the patient. He thought it was just a very bad bruise. But while waiting for his x-ray, I learned there was more to his story that I hadn't heard. When he came back for his follow-up appointment, I asked.

He left Mexico because he could not find work. He is married with four children and had resorted to begging. Tears rolled down his cheeks as he told me. To pay the coyote, he sold his car, the only thing he had of value. That got him the $3,100. Then, in the middle of the desert, the coyote demanded another $1,000, which the man did not have. The smugglers threatened to leave him in the desert or turn him over to a drug cartel at the border. His sister found a way to wire him the money.

"I had to do it," she said. "He's my brother."

When I told him he could not work on his leg and would need to be on crutches, his face fell.

"What's the problem?" I asked.

"I cannot pay for the crutches," he said.

I felt relieved that's all it was. I should have said something sooner. "We will give you the crutches."

Both men would be all right soon enough, but I felt so sick that this is what happened every day on the border of my own country, in order to come to my city. All this money, all this fear, just for the chance not to have to beg in order to feed your children. Yet crossing the Rio Grande breaks American law.

It was in the Jordan River that Jesus knew God's presence. On this issue of caring for immigrants, I am as clear as I can be that I understand what God asks of me. ·

Working for Wellness

The Church Health Center is part of a coalition of organizations redeveloping an old Sears distribution center and retail store known locally as "Crosstown" because of its location, which joins sections of Memphis. In a ninety-year-old building, it was no surprise to discover asbestos that would have to be safely removed. One of the workers helping to do this came to the Church Health Center's walk-in clinic in horrible knee pain at the age of fifty-two. It didn't take long for Scott to tell him he needed knee replacement surgery. Scott's had this procedure himself; he knows it's no piece of cake, but there really was no other option for relieving the man's pain.

"Will I have to miss work?" the man asked.

"Yes."

"I don't know then. The duct tape works pretty good."

The man was taping up his knee every day to go to work. If he doesn't work, he doesn't get paid. He doesn't qualify for any assistance. He doesn't own a house. He is just getting by because he gets up and goes to work every day as long as there is work to be had, no matter how excruciating the pain is in his knee.

Are the people in power listening to stories like this?

Are people of faith listening to stories like this?

How often are we so wrapped up in our own issues that we fail to acknowledge the humanity we share with others?

Are we prepared to respond with kindness?

I was in a conference room with Scott one time when he told a story that should make us all think twice about questions like these. Here's Scott:

· · · · · · · · I taught an adult Sunday school at St. John's for decades after I became an associate pastor there. Richard, who was a physical therapist at the Church Health Center for years, had started a Saturday soup kitchen at the church. For a number of years, Richard was single-handedly in charge. One day he was just worn out and said he couldn't keep doing it on his own. Others in the church would have to step up to keep the soup kitchen open. My Sunday school class decided to take it on. We had people to cook, but we had to get the doors open, set things up, and clean up afterward.

Richard explained we didn't have to worry about the clean-up, though. When the doors opened at 4:00 on Saturday afternoon, the line would be a hundred people long. Right at the front would be Thurman, and Thurman would find two other people who would help with the clean-up. All we had to do was give Thurman six dollars. Each helper would take two dollars. It seemed like a great deal to us. We went on like this for over twelve years. When we arrived to open up, the first question was "Where's Thurman?"

Then one day Thurman was not there. Though he was not a typical street person, I knew he would intermittently abuse substances and binge drink. He was a smart guy, but his issues kept him from holding a steady job. Still, it was unlike him to miss a Saturday.

"Where's Thurman?" I asked my class the next morning.

It turned out Thurman had been found dead on a park bench the night before, overdosed on something.

This is horrible, I thought. *I'm going to his funeral.*

And then it hit me. After twelve years of accepting Thurman's help—expecting it—I had no idea what his last name was. I found him likable as a person when I saw him out and about the neighborhood during the week, but I didn't know his full name.

Thankfully somebody did, and a group of us went to his funeral. But it was unnerving to find myself in that position. Had I taken Thurman for granted all those years and forgotten to be kind? · · · · · · · · · · ·

I hadn't known Scott very long before he arranged for me to go to the Mayo Clinic to have my complicated health issues sorted out and come up with a plan. In the process I discovered that Dr. Bob Waller, who retired in 1999 from his position as CEO at Mayo, had been on the board of the Church Health Center. Dr. Waller started out as an ophthalmologist, but all the senior administrators at Mayo are physicians, and he rose through the ranks. He was the one who made the decision for Mayo to expand to both Jacksonville, Florida, and Scottsdale, Arizona, and widen its network of affiliated hospitals. People on his board at the time thought he might have lost his mental faculties, but great good has come from his daring vision.

Scott met Dr. Waller through a wealthy individual in Memphis who took him to Rochester.

"I had in mind that we were going to meet Dr. Waller and wrestled with how to speak about what we do at the Church Health Center," Scott says. "Dr. Waller came into the room and we talked for a while. When he had to step out to take a phone call, I turned to one of the people with me and said, 'There's no way that guy is the CEO of Mayo. He's too nice.' He was one of the kindest people I've ever met."

Some would argue that Dr. Waller is still one of the most powerful voices in American health care, but you can only be CEO at Mayo for ten years, so he retired at the end of his term. His wife was ready to move home to Memphis, and they did. But Dr. Waller essentially said to Mayo, "I want to help you raise money." He spent a year flying all over the world and single-handedly raised a billion dollars. In Mayo circles, Dr. Waller is affectionately referred to as "the old man."

What an embodiment of the truth that power and kindness in health care do not have to occupy separate orbits that cannot intersect. If we are kind people, will we not also be kind when we have opportunities to change people's lives, including finding that place where faith and health come together for greater wellness in our society?

COMMUNITY CARES

When Scott tells stories about patients, he nearly always uses a name. His patients are not numbers to him. They're people for whom a few minutes of kindness can make an enormous difference.

The year I worked with Reverend Walley, I helped to develop vibrant small groups within the congregation. At the time, the church was in the middle of deciding whether to relocate. The community had become drug infested and was in decline. The question of whether to relocate spun out a variety of camps with a lot of natural opportunity to disagree. The small groups were intended to help people—even those who disagreed—know and be known. We didn't put a lot of other requirements on how they formed, and the people who participated found what they had in common was acts of kindness. People who did not know each other well—or at all—became close friends. Conversations in the church that had been critical turned constructive as people genuinely came to care for each other and pray for each other. True community blossomed in the congregation, and I was amazed at the power of community to change people, to make them confident, to reassure them they were loved.

This story of kindness has two chapters.

This was the congregation that sent me off to seminary. When I finished seminary, I was appointed to a church that averaged about a hundred people on Sunday. When they found out I had HIV, however, they refused to take me. On the night before the scheduled meeting during which I would be introduced as their pastor, the board decided to reject me. In fact, there were threats to burn down the house where I would be living, and they were adamant that I would not be allowed to serve Communion or baptize. The bishop backed down and did not send me there, but now I had no place to go. Pokey and I wanted to return to living near our families.

An older woman, Polly McIntosh, who had been in Reverend Walley's church in the years when I was working with small groups, anonymously donated fifty thousand dollars so that I could have a full-time associate position for two years in the church. She wanted us to be where people could love on us and I could find the security in their kindness to move on from there in my pastoral career. Her only condition was that I not identify her while she was alive, a promise I kept until her death in 2009. Her kindness was such a healing outpouring for us.

If we think of others as numbers and statistics, it's easier to separate power and kindness. When we see others as fellow human beings, flawed and broken and in need of love, and when we know and are known, it's easier to consider our resources and embrace the truth that the person with the power has the responsibility to be kind.

Our God, forgive us for being so focused on our own lives and what happens around us. Open our eyes to a wider world—your world of people you love. Amen.

12

WHEN THE GOING GETS TOUGH

Faith leads the way to health.

Here's Scott:

For twenty-four years I could count on Dr. Raza Dilawari. If I had a patient with cancer and in need of surgery, Raza would do the surgery without a thought about whether the patient could pay his fee. If I had cancer, I would have chosen Raza to treat me. His ability was remarkable.

One day in 2011 my friend operated on a patient for twelve hours. During the surgery, his own stomach was hurting—as it had been for a few weeks. Though he thought it was overkill, he decided to get a CT scan of his abdomen.

He couldn't believe the results. He had pancreatic cancer, and it had spread to his liver. A skilled cancer surgeon had inoperable cancer.

The news spread like wildfire among physicians and hospital staff. Anyone who heard about it felt it in the pit of their stomach—not because one of Memphis's finest surgeons was seriously ill, but because one of our city's finest citizens was suffering.

I sat down with Raza with three cameras rolling. We talked for an hour and a half about the end of life and what it meant to die well.

No question was off limits. We talked matter-of-factly about his disease and the limited options for treatment. He offered advice to future medical students and residents about how to care for people with cancer and other terminal diseases. Raza was soft-spoken and eloquent as we talked about our current moral crisis of letting people die on ventilators around strangers because we do not have the courage to address how dying is a part of life.

Despite his prognosis, Raza still had hope. A Muslim, he proudly proclaimed that he was the only person he knew of who was on the prayer lists of congregations in four different religions. Surely God must be listening!

I had planned to talk with him again on camera, but we didn't have the chance. His pain worsened suddenly. Then in a brief moment, he had a massive stroke. Two days later he was gone.

I know what he would have said to me if we had talked again. "God blessed me with a wonderful wife and children. I wish I could have lived longer to be with them, but it wasn't to be. Many patients have taught me how to die well, and I hope I will follow their example." This is what he believed and how he lived. • • • • • • • • • • • • •

I didn't know Dr. Dilawari, but I certainly admire his courage. While he underwent some treatment for his disease, he did not grasp at minuscule possibilities that an unproven drug or procedure *might* cure him. When I hear his story, I can't help but think that he understood that his death was part of his life, and if he had lived well, he could also die well. And he had the courage to talk about this. While he welcomed prayers, he did not clench his hope around being cured in order to experience healing.

Scott has another moving story about death that is even more personal.

I was seventeen when my mother got sick in the middle of football season. She had surgery, and I remember being told she had ovarian cancer. I didn't understand much about the disease, but the doctor said she would probably live another ten years. As a physician looking back now, I realize that was a ridiculous thing to say. About four months later, she almost died, but rallied and improved. But now they gave us a more realistic prognosis: she would likely live another year. Six months later she clearly was dying, and was admitted to the hospital.

My father and I were holding vigil at her bedside. After he stepped out to speak with the doctor, my father said to me, "Your mom is sleeping. Why don't you go to a movie?"

There was a movie I'd been wanting to see. The theater was only about a mile and a half down the road. My dad handed me a pager and promised to call if anything happened.

I thought she was sleeping. Both the doctor and my father encouraged me to go. So I went.

I was gone barely fifteen minutes when the pager went off. In those days, you had to find a phone to call back on a page. My father told me over the pay phone that in the few minutes I was gone, my mother had died.

She wasn't sleeping. I know now my mother had already entered a stage of breathing where the body is starved for oxygen and death will come soon.

For forty-five years I've felt unease about that decision to go to a movie. I don't exactly feel guilty, but why did I leave? Why did my father let me? He later said he didn't know she was going to die that soon. But mostly the doctor didn't think it was good for me to witness my mother's death, and my father had trusted his opinion.

If I was in the same position with a patient's teenage son, I certainly would not send him to the movies. While I know there was nothing I could have done, my absence at my mother's bedside in that moment is something I have regretted all my life. • • • • • • • • • • • •

How we come to the ends of our earthly lives is a salient and complex issue in our society. All of us hear or read about dire situations, and we might even think, "They should never have put him through that" or "Somebody needs to pull the plug." But of course it's always easier to see the reality that there will be no recovery when it's someone else's mother who is dying. Talking about end-of-life issues is not an easy conversation to have, whether within a family or within a society.

But we must have it.

The Conversation

Think about a few people you've known who died, especially if they were elderly or had long-term illnesses.

Did they die at home in the care of people who loved them, or were they in a hospital surrounded by strangers?

I'm sure we've all known older people—grandparents, great-grandparents, church friends, neighbors—who feel ready to go. They say things like, "I don't understand why I'm still here." Spouses are gone. Friends are gone. Perhaps even children are gone. The body does not work very well, and maybe the mind does not either. Yet if this person has chest pain, someone will call 911, an ambulance will arrive, and at the hospital every effort will be made to forestall a third heart attack. And our elderly loved one remains alive but with an even further diminished quality of life.

At what point do we say that this is not what we want?

At what point do we say that this is not what we want for people we love?

"Too often people spend the last week of their lives in the intensive care unit with a tube stuck down their throat," Scott often says. "They have undergone procedures that had no chance of bringing meaningful improvement, and now they are in a room with fluorescent lights that are never turned off, with caregivers who do not know them well enough to love them. And then they die. It's immoral."

How many of us, of any age, want to die that way?

When we "fight death," who really wins?

I am someone well acquainted with the possibility that my family and I will face decisions about my medical conditions and when "enough is enough."

Growing medical knowledge and technology have brought many benefits to my life, and I am grateful for them. I hope, though, that I will never confuse scientific advances with what it means to find joy and love and significance in living well, regardless of the length of my life.

"The problem is," Scott says, "that our love affair with technology has overpowered our spiritual values. In the last few years, there has been increasing attention paid to end-of-life health care. Unfortunately, the discussion has primarily focused on the cost of care, rather than the morality or theology or ethics of care."

Statistically, many of us will spend 80 percent of our lifetime medical benefits in the last six months of our lives, even when we know that the best we are doing is prolonging the process of dying.

Are we asking the right questions about how to die well? Are we having the right conversations?

Scott points out, "Helping people die well is exactly what churches, synagogues, and mosques are charged to make happen. Yet all too often, decisions about how we die are made entirely by the medical professionals. This must change. Our country must have a national debate led by the faith community about the end of life. Will we all agree? Absolutely not. In fact, there does not need to be only one way to die. But by not having 'the conversation,' we will almost certainly continue to torture those we love."

It's a tough topic. But it's one where people of faith—living in the hope of meaning and significance that faith infuses—are qualified to take the lead.

Faith and Flipping

Maureen Bisognano, president and CEO of the Institute for Healthcare Improvement in Boston, has formulated the challenge of moving from a system that does things *to* patients to one that works *with* patients to achieve the best result for their lives. She calls it "flipping health care." That's a question that applies not only to end-of-life issues but also to how we live well long before the end of life: How can health care help people gain what they truly want from their lives? And if we work together to flip health care so people, rather than technology, are at the center of it, we might find that it becomes easier to answer the end-of-life questions.

And what might be the role of people of faith in this process? Flipping health care helps return health to the purview of faith communities because it recognizes the nonclinical needs and goals of the individual and the ways that clinical care can be aligned with how the patient identifies meaning.

Congregations should be grasping for this opportunity! This is a chance to bear witness to how the spiritual dimensions of our lives play a defining role in health not because of a mysterious "faith healing" cure that comes on the heels of prayer but because of a larger vision of the wholeness that comes when we see meaning and significance woven through all of life, even illness and suffering—and even death. We should not hesitate to lead the way in dialogue and example.

Here's a great story from Scott about the quality of our living:

Over the years a number of doctors have retired and called to offer us their used medical equipment. Often the equipment is fifty years old and looks like it should have been replaced years ago. One day a few years back I went to talk to a doctor who was retiring and wanted to give us his exam tables.

My level of expectation was low.

"My father also used these tables," he said. "They were built in 1926."

He was not helping his case.

To my great surprise, although the tables were seventy years old, they were made of beautiful mahogany and were in excellent condition. They even had matching wooden trash cans. The tables had been made with such quality and had been so well cared for that I was sure they would last another seventy years.

The issue of quality was brought home to me when two patients came to see me on the same morning. Both were likely to die soon. The first was a woman with breast cancer that had spread. She had made peace and did not appear anxious as she explained that her main concern was living her remaining days with as much meaning as she could. The other was a man with prostate cancer. He was prepared for death; he just hoped he'd be able to fish a while longer.

For both of them, the quality of their lives mattered. They wanted to live their lives to the end with the same enduring quality as those mahogany exam tables.

Faith communities have huge assets to bring to the health table. Perhaps we participate in the general culture so fully that we neglect to see the ways we can enrich it precisely because of our faith. Congregations often bring together people from various neighborhoods in a city and from various career paths and income brackets. All of these people come with their own networks—family, neighborhood, workplace, exercise groups, service organizations, and so on.

Can you see where we're going?

People of faith have theological and ethical reasons to think differently about complicated issues, but they also have wide opportunity to influence social conversations at multiple levels. We need to be willing to think outside the box.

The Church Health Center engages tough questions by leveraging the faith community to reach people who need help, creating opportunities for people of faith to participate in the work, and by influencing the way people of faith understand health and are positioned to speak out in public discourse.

Scott never hesitates to speak out on the role people of faith can play, especially among Christians who share his language of faith. His words of advice focus on three main areas where communities of faith can speak with a clear voice on the subject of health care.

First, reclaim the body. The body is not the purview of science with nothing to do with theology. That is the voice of culture hearkening all the way back to Plato, but Plato was wrong about this. We believe that no matter what we do to our bodies, when they break, the doctors can use technology to fix them. But technology is not that good, and the doctor is not that smart. God gave us our bodies for a reason, and we have an obligation to care for them. We must reclaim the body as rightfully belonging to conversations of faith.

Second, reclaim life. Daily life is full of choices that soon enough become habits. Congregational life is full of traditions we soon enough stop questioning. People of faith have an opportunity to come alongside individuals in changing habits and decision patterns. Imagine what might happen if churches began to ask, "Is this program—this tradition, this snack, this meal—helping people live healthy lives as God intends, or is it a stumbling block to their efforts?" Churches have the potential to be powerhouses of life-giving community. We must reclaim a priority of life as God intends, rather than the life our culture delivers.

Third, reclaim death. Yes, claim death. We, as the people of God, have not spoken up about how we understand the end of life. We have allowed a relentless application of technology to prolong life at all costs. The death of our physical existence is not the enemy. Christians should be the first ones to embrace this truth. Even Jesus, whom Christians believe to be God's Son, shared the human experience of death. Christians believe that death does not have the last word, but it is often hard to see this expression of faith in the health decisions we make.

As people of faith become more vocal in the discussion of health care that has become an albatross around the public neck, they can speak up on practical solutions. A complex question such as the end of life is only one neglected area in the public square. What do we even mean by the term *health care reform*? Acting out of an experience of what it means to be connected to God, and formed by God's love, people of faith should not underestimate the impact they could make by calling the conversation about health care reform back to an essential understanding of what it means to be healthy not just clinically but in all dimensions of life.

What might happen if people of faith were, on a large scale, to rethink models of health care that go beyond emergency care for the poor? The hospitals of history have already succumbed to the economic "survival of the fittest" model. Hospitals all over the country retain church names but no longer belong to denominations. But what about a new model? Draw from the gifts and passions of the faith community to carry the light beyond the end of the church parking lot.

And what if we work for prevention at every level of our shared society? Get involved in community movements that can improve the socioeconomic indicators of poverty at the local level—education, housing, race relations, employment, justice. Washington cannot do this. Not even state capitals can do this. It takes people who know and care about a specific community.

Communities of faith must keep the door to conversation open, rather than slam it shut when the answers are not black and white. The questions will be tough, but faith is what it will take to bring conversation back to talking about improved health outcomes, rather than how to pay for a broken system.

The time to grasp life is not in the desperate moments before death, but in the moments that happen every day in every community across the country. Rather than saying, "Doctor, do everything you can" when we fear the separation death will bring or the absence it creates, we would serve each other more fully and with more healing by saying to each other, "Do everything you can" to bathe every life in love and significance.

COMMUNITY CARES

Because I live with serious health issues, you might wonder if things turn morbid at my house every time I get sick. The answer is no. Not even close.

My grandfather used to say that the death rate hovers right around 100 percent for all of us. Not a single person is *not* going to die. But we do tend to cope with that truth in different ways, some of them better than others.

In my mind, it's a gift to my family that my children have known their whole lives about issues of living and death. We've had lots of conversations about how life is fragile and about making every day count. Every day matters. Because the day matters, you matter. When I die, or when Pokey dies, my children will feel no less grief or no less anxiety about what the passing means for their lives. But what they do have, right now, is a true appreciation for the day, for every moment, for every memory. That becomes their source of comfort, and that is beauty.

Some people live a lot of years, but they don't live a lot of moments. The tragedy of life is not that one day we will die, but that sometimes we take so long to realize it's time to live. One of the things faith allows is for us to not only be able to look at the whole of life from one frame to the next—with a beginning, a middle, and an end—but also to talk about it in terms that are hopeful.

We humans are grouped in many different ways, such as families, including what Scott calls "chosen family," neighborhoods, work groups, congregations, even entire towns or cities. Some of our groupings are voluntary; we choose to belong to them. Others result from various circumstances or factors that we have less control over. Consider how many groups you are part of in the various dimensions of life. Some groups can suck the life out of us. We all know that experience. On the other hand, when we put people together who value life together and interact in loving ways, the group becomes a life-giving agent.

Think about the values that faith brings to the way we understand life and love and joy and even death. Let the conversation about the tough issues begin there, and faith will lead the way to health.

Our God, we would rather stay in the spot where we are comfortable, where we know what to expect and where we are not challenged by your new ways. Forgive us for our unwillingness to go where we are called. Help us to act in the name of your justice, wherever it leads us. Amen.

13

SUFFER THE LITTLE CHILDREN

Education is a health issue.

Here's Scott:

In 1997, the principal of a Memphis elementary school came to me and asked us to start a health clinic in her school. Initially I had no interest in doing that, but before she left that day she said to me, "The children don't feel well."

It is not possible to walk away from children who do not feel well, so we began a small clinic in her school.

We soon learned that the health problems of the children in the school ran far deeper than the services we were providing. Early on, Lirah, the principal, told me an unsettling story.

"What's your name?" a teacher asked a first grader.

"Peanut," he replied.

"No, what's your real name?"

Silence. A boy in first grade did not know his name. This was just the surface indication of how unprepared he was for interacting with the world and engaging in learning. And the number-one predictor of a child's long-term health is the education he or she receives. If children reach school age without the most fundamental preparation for learning, what will their futures hold in terms of health?

From a medical point of view, we can either treat Peanut as he grows up for the variety of problems that will develop because of his poor early childhood development and education, or we can help him get a better start. Education is a health care issue, and it's one we can do something about. ·

With the help of an extremely generous donor, the Church Health Center set out to make a difference. Two years after that initial conversation with the principal, they opened Perea, a charter preschool that meets in a public school building.

In the time of Jesus, Perea was a region east of the Jordan River. On his final journey to Jerusalem where he would soon be crucified, Jesus encountered a group of children. Against the inclination of his closest followers, he chose to bless the children, saying, "Let the little children come to me, and do not stop them; for it is to such as these that the kingdom of heaven belongs" (Matt. 19:14).

Jesus cared about the children. That's a pretty good reason for us to do the same.

When the first class of three-year-olds entered Perea, every one of them tested below the tenth percentile on a national standardized test. Fifteen years later, when they graduated from high school, many of them were headed to college with scholarships and ready to take the world by storm. The Church Health Center made a difference, and every year a new group of three-year-olds enters Perea with a brighter future ahead of them because they are there. Every year is a new beginning. In each year's entering class of three-year-olds, about 65 percent of the children are delayed or very delayed in basic areas like numbers, letters, and shapes. But just two years later, 90 percent of the same group of children score average or advanced. Perea also requires parents to be involved in the school and teaches children essential life skills such as self-regulation, problem solving, concentration, and conflict resolution. The school has a waiting list of more than twice the number of students it can accommodate.

Education is on the radar of the Church Health Center, and the blip is moving steadily toward the center. Education is an effective first step toward changing poverty levels, which will lead to better health outcomes over a lifetime.

Preschools are not the only place to target education that will lead to healthier lives.

"I could solve 90 percent of the problems I deal with every day in one way," Scott says. "Give people better jobs. If we could eliminate poverty, not all the problems we deal with would go away, because we're all going to die, but a lot of them would get better."

The link between better education and better-paying jobs won't surprise anyone. But those of us with insurance cards in our pockets and checking accounts to cover premiums and co-pays may live at a distance from the reality that poverty, including educational opportunities, is an underlying cause of poor health outcomes. When we talk about access to health care, we tend to think in terms of affordable insurance and enough primary care physicians to go around. We think less about the social issues that get in the way of health and wellness.

Inadequate public transportation systems that make it impossible for low-income individuals without cars or gas money to get to appointments—or to get to a job that would pay a higher wage.

Locations that do not require taking half a day off work, without pay, to see a doctor.

Stores that sell little food other than boxed and processed products, yet may be the only ones a family can get to.

Literacy levels insufficient to read and understand basic health information and instructions.

Neighborhoods where it is unsafe for children to be outside.

Isolation from recreational spaces.

Along with classrooms filled with students achieving far below standards, these are all signs of poverty, and they all impact health.

Don't we want better for our children? Don't we want the next generation to look back and see that they live in a stronger, healthier community?

Education is a strategic place to start—at every level.

Hope at Risk

National politics of health care and education dominate public discourse. The two challenges are not as independent of each other as we might imagine. People with more education seem to have less risk of heart disease and diabetes, for instance. They are also more likely to engage in positive health behaviors. Research continues to explore whether people with more education have lower rates of dementia when they are older.

At a dinner a few years ago, Scott hosted a table of brand-new Memphis City Schools teachers. In the process, he conversed with the former editor of the Penn State newspaper, the president of the senior class at Florida State, and a member of the women's crew team at the University of Michigan. Everyone was impressive and everyone was excited about being in Memphis.

Scott was invited to the event because the Church Health Center was exploring a partnership with Teach for America. This is a concrete example of joining forces with the gifts that others bring to the table. Teach for America places teachers in inner-city and rural schools that are under-resourced and where the students have complicated lives that put them at risk of not performing at grade level—like the three-year-olds coming into Perea, who already are far below the national standards of development. One in three of the sixteen million kids growing up in poverty will not graduate from high school. Only 9 percent of those graduates will have earned a bachelor's degree by the time they're twenty-five. Teach for America teachers commit to two years in schools serving at-risk populations to make a difference not just for a school year but quite possibly for a child's lifetime.

Early intervention will help. Preschool is the right place to begin. But the Church Health Center is also excited to partner with Teach for America for two other reasons. First, the Church Health Center's interest in education will not stop with getting preschoolers ready for kindergarten. Their work in education will expand, because education is such a clear pathway to better health. Working with charter schools for elementary and high school students will help keep kids on the road to full lives where they will more likely make healthy choices.

Second, at the end of two years, members of Teach for America look at where they want their own lives to go. Many continue as teachers. Others enter varied fields—medical school, law school, politics, business. And if this happens, now we have future doctors, lawyers, politicians, and business leaders who have seen up close the social and educational issues that keep the playing field so uneven. And isn't that a good thing? Whatever fields they enter, Teach for America teachers can be advocates for education with the voice of experience.

Education is a health issue. What I love about the Church Health Center on this question is that they aren't just waving around the considerable evidence of this conclusion from the safety of a clinic. They're putting skin in the game, and they keep putting more skin in the game. Education opens the door to wider conversations about socioeconomic factors that affect the health of the next generation.

People of faith have a heritage that connects learning to well-being. The Old Testament, particularly Psalms and Proverbs, is full of descriptions of learning from teaching and experiencing improved well-being in the process. Jesus was a teacher to crowds and small groups. His disciples became teachers. Paul wrote about the spiritual gift of teaching. The Bible honors the truth that God created humans as learning beings who move closer to God.

We talked earlier about hope and its connection to well-being. We need to see that something else is possible beyond the circumstances we find ourselves in, often through no fault of our own. The line that connects education and hope is an obvious one.

Scott often has opportunity to speak to audiences of young adults—college or medical students, for instance. He plays on a dream angle in these settings because students are understandably thinking about their futures. "If you have a dream you're committed to—that is more than a fanciful notion—you can make it work," he says. "Other people will want to see it happen. My dream was always around what it means in today's world to have a healing ministry." Speaking about his own life's work challenges listeners to reflect on how their dreams can make their communities stronger and more caring. While education is a path out of ingrained poverty and leads to better health for individuals over their lifetimes, can it also lead to better health for communities?

It can if we begin to dream of a different future. Early-childhood education prepares children to be lifelong learners with greater control over their own futures. A new brand of medical education can prepare physicians to be lifelong learners who practice medicine differently than previous generations.

Moving toward Empathy

An educational dimension most people don't experience as students is medical school. On the other hand, we *do* experience the results of medical education every time we see a physician or undergo a test, so we have a vested interest in the shape of medical education.

"Almost universally," Scott says, "the reason people go to medical school is that they want to help people." But they creep over to the dark side, what Scott calls the "religion of medicine." It's part of the training. Don't get attached. Stay objective. Stick to the scientific evidence.

Scott speaks to groups of medical students fairly often. He knows how easily young people who entered medical school because they wanted to help people can get sucked into operating strictly on science and separating themselves from a personal connection with the people they care for. In fact, he frequently tells his own story of realizing this was happening to him. He says:

Once when I was a third-year medical student, I was doing CPR compressions on a patient while a resident was running the code. In the middle of what clearly was an emergency, someone stuck a head in and said, "Hey, when the code is over, where are we going for pizza?" And I began to think, *Do I want pepperoni or mushrooms?* Then I said to myself, *What has happened to me? This is not why I want to be a doctor.* This was a real human being under my hands. He was probably going to die, because even our great medical skills were not bringing him back. And I was thinking about pizza? Something was terribly askew.

"We have an unholy love affair with technology," Scott will often say. We have trained both physicians and patients to depend on technology and value the newest forms above understanding each other's lives and embracing elements as basic as love and empathy.

"How can I create an educational system that brings more love into the world?" Scott asks. "If you can do that, you win."

The Medical College Admission Test (MCAT) now contains questions relating to human behavior and psychology. Being a physician is not just about science. The very human experience of empathy leads to more satisfied patients, improved health outcomes, and lower burnout rates among doctors.

One study shows that doctors, on average, interrupt a patient within eighteen seconds of when the patient begins speaking. When our children do that, we use it as a teachable moment for them to learn about respect for the person they are interrupting. So medical schools are beginning to include required coursework that teaches new physicians to listen better and to do something as basic as making eye contact with the patient rather than only looking at the electronic screen where they are ticking off boxes and making notes.

"I don't care how much medical students learn," Scott says. "When someone comes to them with a broken heart, they can MRI the heart all day long and they will never know what love looks like. If they're not trying to figure out that this is part of taking care of patients, they're going to miss the boat."

And then he tells medical students, "It is possible to come back from the dark side. I promise you it is."

Scott is extending hands to pull people back and offer another path through a career in medicine—one that lets doctors help people by seeing a medical situation in the context of the life where it occurs. In partnership with Baptist Hospital in Memphis, the Church Health Center now has a residency in family practice program, and residents are encouraged, rather than discouraged, to understand the bigger picture of a patient's life and not to reduce the physician-patient relationship to test results and "you should" conversations. When residents leave the program, they'll have hands-on experience with a different sort of medical practice and their own vision to practice medicine in a way that responds to the health toll of broken hearts, not just broken bodies.

The residency program will cycle back to a relationship with Teach for America. Many alumni of Teach for America end up in top medical schools. Their experience in urban settings primes them to be social entrepreneurs, with medicine as a path to helping build a stronger community. Now those teachers can train as doctors in a setting that practices values that result in community transformation.

COMMUNITY CARES

Education is a health care issue for all of us. Are our youngest children prepared to learn well and experience a hope-filled life? Are the doctors we trust to care for us prepared to learn and practice well? And are we, as patients, prepared to understand the factors within our control that contribute to our experience of health and the ways we nurture wellness in each other? Most of us have some learning to do. We can learn to see Peanut as a human being who deserves to experience the fullness of life with hope. We can learn to appreciate that some elements of life that we take for granted, the social determinants of health, become barriers to health when they are missing from someone else's life, or from entire neighborhoods or communities. We can learn that respect for another person's dignity is an essential ingredient to well-being. Education is not merely a program that funds classrooms; it's also mutual participation in the societal learning curve that will lead to better health on a larger scale.

Everybody has a passion for something, whether it's teaching or medicine or social work or another field that brings strength to a community. Part of the work of a community is to help its members discover what they are passionate about and create paths that take them there. Education is a path.

Even beyond passion is the truth that every person has some kind of gift—something to contribute to the community in which the person lives or the groups to which the person belongs. If we begin to see that our gifts are not only for our own benefit but ultimately for the well-being of the society we share, we have changed the game to a higher level. Education can do this.

The important role of the community is to help people marry their passions with their contributable gifts—both to be excited about something and to know that it has value at a level larger than individual experience. The more we do this through all forms of education at all levels of learning, the greater difference we will see in health and wellness. Faith communities need not separate education and health ministry as if they do not overlap. Education is a health issue, and it's one we can do something about.

> *Our God, we proclaim that you are love, yet we all too often do not know love. Forgive us for not being more serious about love. Commit us to listening to love, practicing love, and making love our aim. Amen.*

14

GROWING UP WITH HOPE AND HEALING

Invest in the young.

This is one of my favorite stories from Scott:

Menachem is a young African American man who grew up in Tupelo, Mississippi. He was born at the time of the Camp David Accords under President Carter, and his mother was so enamored of the prospect of peace in the Middle East that she was determined to name her son Anwar, Jimmy, or Menachem. The family was poor, but Menachem turned out to be a gifted football player and earned a scholarship to Rhodes College in Memphis. He played hard and studied hard, with the dream of going to medical school.

He didn't get in the first time he applied, so he became a clinic assistant at the Church Health Center. That's how I met him. He worked forty hours a week for us, and he had a second job as a bouncer at a nightclub. One Sunday night my wife and I ran into him in a record store, which turned out to be his third job. Mary and I fell in love with Menachem and took him under our wing.

When Menachem got into med school, I sat down with him and said, "You realize you can't work while you're in med school." I'd been to med school. I knew the realities.

He answered, "But I've been working since I was eleven."

"What did you do when you were eleven?"

"I collected garbage on the back of a truck before school."

Menachem's work ethic never ceases to amaze me.

I made the really big mistake—because my plan was for him to come back to work at the Church Health Center—of taking Menachem to the Big Apple, and he fell in love with New York. He ended up matching with Beth Israel for his residency.

Beth Israel's clinic serves a large population of Hasidic Jews. The doctors who see them are residents. Patients look at a list of names and pick who is going to be their doctor, often without knowing anything more about the doctors. Menachem! What Hasidic Jew is not going to say, "I'm picking Menachem!"

When it first happened, patients were very surprised to meet Menachem, and Menachem had no idea what a Hasidic Jew was. Then he was doing his family practice obstetrics rotation, and a woman was in labor. Menachem was caring for her, and the father was pacing constantly around the room, looking at his watch and asking Menachem how long it was going to take.

Menachem is sort of a laid-back guy, and he said, "Look, hang on, it's going to happen."

Finally, the father said, "So, look, are you going to get the baby out by Shabbat?"

Perhaps you don't know what Shabbat is. The Jewish Sabbath starts at sunset on Friday.

"Are you going to get the baby out by Shabbat?" Menachem had no ability to answer that question. First of all, he didn't know what Shabbat was, and second, it wasn't up to him when the baby would come. When Menachem finally figured it out, all of a sudden he was closer to being on the same page as the father. I'm not sure the father was ever on Menachem's page, but while Menachem could not speed up the birth, he now had a cultural understanding that the father was anxious that the baby wouldn't come before the Sabbath began and work should cease.

Menachem stayed on in New York after his residency, and patients now choose him not because of his name but because they know the kind of doctor he is. They know he has taken the time and effort to learn what Hasidism is all about. It makes him a better doctor. •

Scott invested in a young man who has learned a powerful tool for being a doctor that people trust. I can appreciate the difference that made because of my experience of Reverend Walley mentoring me when I was a college student and I first began to work in a congregation. In fact, I've always had a Reverend Walley at various crucial points in my life. As I live through ages and stages, mentors have been there, including a pediatrician who cared for me when I was a child and became my good friend. Even now, as a senior pastor, I have strong relationships with members in the congregation. Although I am their pastor, they are my mentors.

We're never too old to learn, and we're never too young to teach.

Sometimes this kind of mentoring is intentional. Sometimes it happens as a bonus to what we're undertaking. Scott received this letter:

My name is Toye Bogard. My father, who is now deceased, was Leroy Bogard. He was one of your long-time patients. He loved you!

When I was growing up, my father used to take me to Hope & Healing Center. I loved the place and purpose so much that I wrote a business plan when I was sixteen.

Well, two years ago, I started a group called Fit Nation. We are a community-based group, with the main purpose of building relationships, having fun, and getting fit.

In two years we have lost over four thousand pounds! We are 6,300 members strong in six states. We filed for our 501(c)3 status. I'm so excited. I just wanted you to know how your vision indirectly sparked my vision within Fit Nation.

Interns and Scholars

If you look around the Church Health Center, you see young people everywhere. Child Life Education and Movement welcomes children into Church Health Wellness—kids like Toye who come with their parents and absorb the culture.

And then there are the interns. Every fall, spring, and summer semester of the academic year, more college students apply for unpaid internships with the Church Health Center than the organization can possibly handle. College students explore their passions and dip their toes into fields they may some day enter with a degree in hand. Interns representing students across the social and science spectrums are scattered throughout the organization, where they work alongside employees, receive on-the-job training, and complete special projects to develop skills they will carry forward. And of course it's an opportunity for them to absorb the culture of a place where faith is in action at every turn. The Church Health Center has a chance to help form their world views and influence how a new generation hears the call to be a healing presence in their communities.

Some of these students may even come back after college in another competitive program: Church Health Scholars.

Within the first few years the Church Health Center was open, an ophthalmologist volunteered by seeing patients with cataracts. One day he called Scott and said his son couldn't get into medical school because he'd had a recurring substance-abuse problem. So Scott took the young man under his wing, had him work in the clinic, and did what he could to help him get into medical school. That young man became an outstanding ophthalmologist who took over the family practice.

The clinic assistant program that began with that young man evolved into a program with requirements and an application process. These students have distinguished themselves with nearly perfect grade point averages in college, and many of them are headed to graduate school. But first they want a year to help bring their futures into focus, a year of "real life" in an employment setting. Their GPAs testify that they have figured out how to study and conquer book learning. Now they're looking for another kind of learning. And it's not about money. While they receive health insurance, scholars are paid very little. They are there for the work experience and the discerning process the year allows them.

"It's not about free labor," Scott says. "It's about shaping and nurturing. I want to be their mother—I don't want to tell them what to do, but I want to be watching, and if they are about to go off track I can just bat them back on the path."

At first, scholars were all clinic assistants. Most of them, like Menachem, had in mind going to medical school and thought the scholar year would give them a better understanding of the medical world. Hundreds of clinic assistants have gone on to become doctors, and many have joined specialty practices in Memphis and now volunteer for the Church Health Center. They become the oncologists or gynecologists or radiologists or pediatricians eager to rejoin the mission of the Church Health Center with expertise the organization needs.

One young woman came from Gambia to attend college in the United States with the goal of eventually going to medical school. After her scholar year, she went on to earn a master's in public health before med school. Her goal is to become a gynecologist and return to Gambia, where she will be the first female gynecologist in the country—and only the second physician with this specialty.

As the program matured, it opened to students who might or might not be aiming toward medical school. Now there are scholars throughout the organization, working alongside staff in areas such as magazine design, visual communications, resource distribution, development, and child education. Some may head to seminary or decide to earn a degree in nonprofit management. While they're in Memphis they see how an entire organization contributes to the health of a community and learn that health and wellness are not restricted to people with medical training, but are a table to which we all bring our gifts. Along with their work responsibilities, Church Health Scholars complete required reading, write reflections on what they are learning, and participate in debates on topics related to issues of social justice and health care.

In Their Words

Every July a new batch of scholars arrives for a year of hard work. Here is some of the evidence of how this phenomenal investment in the young will reap rewards for the communities where the scholars choose to build their lives.

Chris: As a clinic assistant, humility is almost forced upon you. You are the low man (or woman) on the totem pole, and a large portion of the grunt work falls to you. And when it comes time to do that work, you have two options. You can either think of yourself as "too good for this" and angrily suffer through whatever it is you are doing, or you can realize that you're not too good for anything, count yourself lucky for all you've been given, and be thankful for the opportunity to serve others through your work in the mission of the Church Health Center. The first option leads to bitterness and resentment. The second leads to joy and fulfillment. I think this is part of what Dr. Morris is trying to tell us when he says that putting on humility will be good for our health.

Jordan: My experience at the Church Health Center clinic has served as a guide to examine my deepest motivations. What I found is that I'm not perfect. Even in the process of caring for Memphis's uninsured workers I still get frustrated, annoyed, and agitated. I fail to perfectly embody the original physician's mentality that Jesus demonstrated. However, I have also found that I am growing. I truly desire to see equality in health care, and I enjoy the role I get to play as a clinic assistant. These past months have exponentially grown my vision for faith-based health care. I want to be a doctor more now than ever, and I can see that I am beginning to develop the sacrificial heart that accompanies effective physicians.

Christopher: My purpose for pursuing the field of medicine is evolving now more than ever through my work at the Church Health Center. While working as a clinic assistant I am truly experiencing the importance of God's mission to heal the sick. Furthermore, I am seeing firsthand how there are so many underprivileged people who do not have access to the health care that they need and deserve. Within the first couple of weeks at the Church Health Center, this fact was engraved into my mind. I checked in a patient who had recently lost health insurance at her job. This lady had HIV, and she had been without her medication for *months*. That is when it clicked. She was at a stage with the virus where she *had* to have her medication in order to live healthily. Yet because of her low income and social status, she did not have access to the care she needed. With each day at the Church Health Center, God is pushing me to intertwine my faith and work. I feel called to delve deeper into Scripture and deeper into my vocation of healing the sick.

COMMUNITY CARES

When I hear stories like this from young people who are engaging with their own faith, whatever it may be, and beginning to frame their futures around issues of equality in health care and a holistic understanding of what it means to be healthy individuals or to have healthy communities, my pulse picks up! There are doctors resisting the pattern of separating their faith from a life's work in the field of healing. Young people are learning virtues like humility by staring straight into what it means to be willing to serve others. They're learning compassion by holding the hands of people who need a healing touch. All around them are ideas that challenge them not only to ferret out what they think about health and wellness issues for a society but also to see the shape of their place in the cultural conversation.

And that excites me. When we invest in the young, we invest in the people who will lead health change in the future.

What can faith communities do to invest in the next generation so that society can be well and whole?

First, value young people. Sometimes we tend to subjugate young people, pushing them off to one side or to their own programs. Then we wonder why they don't want to do the things we think they should do. This creates an adversarial dynamic between one generation and the next. Instead, let's see children, youth, and younger adults as full members of our faith communities. As we talk about these issues in our settings, may we be mindful of ways to invite young people into the room and to the table, not just in a special meeting but as a habitual practice. In the congregation I serve now, we try to be intentional about including young people in vital conversations and listening to their voices.

Second, we can do a better job of modeling the learner-teacher experience. We're all learning, and we all have ways to teach. A person's youth—which is a relative notion to begin with—does not mean they are not capable and eager to be active in what the congregation is doing. Look at skills and personality. If we look only at age, we risk cutting off an entire generation. We invest in the young when we recognize that they do in fact have something to teach us and that we do in fact have something to learn from them.

God of us all, you breathe life into each of us, and we are all different. We each see the world through our own eyes. Lead us to find ways to join hands and run or walk the marathon of this life. Give us courage to fight the good fight and to go forth to make love and justice the core of our being. Amen.

15

IF YOUR HEART IS LIKE MY HEART

Touch the heart and soul of humanity.

Here's Scott:

On the street outside St. John's United Methodist Church, across the street from the Church Health Center, are park benches the church installed for people waiting for the bus or who are just tired. Every day Philip spent much of his day sitting on one of those benches. I was not quite sure why he was there or what he was thinking. He was in his mid-fifties, but he'd had a stroke. Several times a day he went for a walk, slowly crossing the street, walking around our parking lot, and returning to the bench.

I'd been his doctor for a few years and learned a few things about him. Philip was a simple man, very kind and asking little of others. He was easy to care for, because he didn't complain or express his needs. Every day I said hello and wished him a good day. Once or twice I came upon him urinating against our building. He was embarrassed when I tried to explain it was okay if he needed to come inside to use the toilet.

One Sunday just before Christmas, after church, Philip was in his usual spot, but he seemed anxious. He was standing up and looking down the street expectantly.

After I was in my car and beginning to drive home, I saw Joy and Scott, a couple from my Sunday school class, helping Philip put on a new overcoat. In late December, even in Memphis, it gets quite cold, especially if you spend your days sitting on a park bench. Joy zipped up the coat, and Philip beamed.

The next day I looked out my office window, which overlooks the street. Under the tree, on the bench, was Philip. He was the same as always—except for his new coat.

Philip's world and the world of Joy and Scott are nothing alike, except for the bench in front of the church, which has brought them together.

God gives all of us a few chances to touch the heart and soul of simple humanity. I was glad I could see it happen before my eyes. • • • • • •

A couple of years ago a young art history professor made an appointment to see Scott in his office. Todd Richardson was involved with an organization known as Crosstown Arts, with a vision for revitalizing an old building for the Memphis arts community. These were early days of envisioning the process of turning a massive former Sears distribution center, which had been empty for decades, into what Richardson called a "vertical urban village." Art and art-related activities would be the main themes for how the building was redeveloped, with the belief that this theme would attract businesses and organizations that wanted to support art and valued the contribution art made in the community. Crosstown would be a mix of art residencies, working studios in a variety of media, and exhibition space. Artists would live on the premises and be involved with the local neighborhood. What Todd wanted to know was whether the Church Health Center would be interested in opening a satellite clinic. Working artists are often in the category of "working uninsured" that the Church Health Center serves, and others in the surrounding neighborhood certainly were part of that population as well.

Scott made a decision in about sixty seconds.

Scott once had the opportunity to carry the Olympic torch. He was not a young athlete anymore, and he already lived with severe joint pain. But this was an opportunity he just couldn't pass up. Knowing it would be the last time he would ever run, even for a quarter of a mile, Scott injected his own knee with pain medication and arranged multiple braces on his legs.

He was going to carry the torch, and he was going to run.

Sometimes we have to do the stuff that seems crazy. An opportunity plops down in front of you, and you just have to say yes.

As Scott listened to Todd's brief pitch about a vertical urban village, he saw much more than a satellite clinic. He saw the future home of the Church Health Center. He saw a "for such a time as this" moment. Scott took the idea and began to run.

If Your Heart Is like My Heart

When Sears Crosstown opened in 1927, more than thirty thousand people came to celebrate a grand day in Memphis. In the building's heyday, Sears employed thousands of Memphians in the retail store or the catalog order fulfillment center. It was also the place of dreams. It was where kids went to sit on Santa's lap and where parents bought their kids' first bikes. Many people purchased their first washing machines there or had their first look at a color television.

Families went to Sears as a recreational togetherness activity. Most important, it touched every segment of society. Black, white, rich, poor, North Memphis, East Memphis—Sears Crosstown brought families together. In 1965, the final addition was completed. But by 1983, Sears had closed the retail store, and ten years later the whole site shut down.

The building began to deteriorate in the way that empty structures do, even iconic ones. Graffiti was scrawled on the walls inside and out. Windows broke. The roof leaked and water collected. Metal chutes and conveyor systems, abandoned when Sears left, rusted. Year after year, it remained vacant. A community icon was becoming a community albatross. Even tearing it down to make room for something modern and useful would cost a small fortune.

In the same era that the Memphis building went up, Sears opened ten similar sites around the country. Chicago, Kansas City, and Philadelphia opted to tear down their structures. But Atlanta, Boston, Dallas, Minneapolis, and Seattle chose to renovate theirs to make them viable for commercial purposes. Minneapolis's structure houses a popular mall, and in Seattle, the Starbucks headquarters occupies the giant building. Only Los Angeles and Memphis were left. Working with Crosstown Arts and a pair of wealthy citizens who had bought the building, Todd had approached hundreds of potential tenants who could occupy space at Crosstown and help support both the arts and a revitalized neighborhood. Most wished him well but didn't see themselves as taking on such a dubious commitment.

In that sixty-second flash of insight while he listened to Todd Richardson, Scott saw that the revitalization of this building would have the effect for the next generation that Sears had when it drew people from all over.

Scott said no to a satellite clinic.

He said yes to moving all of the Church Health Center's bursting-at-the-seams operations to Crosstown.

The Church Health Center had been wrestling for years with what to do about its inadequate space for employees and how they could serve more of the thousands of people on their waiting lists, and serve them better. Until now, the strategy had been to find yet another building, usually old repurposed houses. But as the Center grew, this approach stretched both resources and organizational culture. Scott could have led the charge for the Church Health Center to raise money to construct its own brand-new campus. Instead he led the charge to go full in at Crosstown.

The truth is, it would have been cheaper to build from scratch, but moving to Crosstown was more than getting new space. It was putting skin in the game.

For all of its history, the Church Health Center had been looking for fresh and effective ways to engage with the local community around themes of whole-person health. Scott's own understanding of the social determinants of health had grown exponentially, reinforcing his conviction that we cannot be healthy apart from community.

Faith communities.

Exercise communities.

Learning communities.

Business communities.

Medical communities.

All of these functioned and interconnected within Memphis, but they were still separate.

What if they were neighbors—good neighbors? What if they knew each other's stories and understood what they each brought to the table? What if living together would help them understand each other better? What if this was *exactly* what was needed to leverage all the resources of the city in a way that could make a profound difference, the likes of which Memphis had never seen?

This was the Church Health Center's chance to practice what it had been preaching for all of its history, and not from the shelter of its own location but in and with other organizations taking the same leap into the vertical urban village.

The Church Health Center quickly became one of the founding partners and a major organizer for Crosstown.

"We put all our eggs in the basket of moving to Crosstown," Scott says. "It will be the coolest building in Memphis. It's driven by the young. It's everything that is about the future of Memphis, and we'll be right in the middle of that."

The Church Health Center is the tenant that occupies the most space at Crosstown, but the vertical urban village also includes several other medical organizations, charter schools all the way through high school, a Goodwill Excel Center that helps adults earn high school diplomas, and opportunities for local college students to engage in learning and service. Memphis Teacher Residency will house and train up to a hundred teachers on the premises. Crosstown Arts will run an artist-residency program, art-making labs, and performance and exhibition spaces. Medical residents in the Church Health Center's family will live alongside people they serve.

"We can't be healthy in isolation," Scott says. "We can't do it alone. We need each other. This applies not just to individuals but to organizations. We have to be in relationship with each other and develop a healthy way of being, corporately as well as individually."

Patients at the Church Health Center are able to move smoothly from clinic appointments to nutrition classes or life coaching in the Wellness facility. Staff are able to walk low-income workers lacking a high school diploma to the Goodwill Excel Center to learn about enrolling. Anyone who visits the location for any reason is able to enjoy art in action.

Mix young doctors in with artists and educators to see what happens. That's what Scott wants to do. He calls it a "cauldron of creativity," convinced that the experience will make for better doctors, more engaged social entrepreneurs, and healthier communities.

"One of the worst things that happens to doctors is that their social skills become incredibly sad," Scott says. "All they can do is talk about medicine and an interesting case. They don't talk about movies. If you're not a well-rounded individual, what gives you the right to advise others how to live their lives?

"This leads to doctors becoming incredibly bored with work. They have high divorce rates, spend money like water, and need expensive toys. They're not going to be good at anything that requires human interaction. Ultimately that leads to high suicide rates among doctors. In the general population, suicide among men is four times the rate of women, and among physicians the rates are the same. Giving young doctors—and teachers—this experience of seeing a community bound together will pay off in the years ahead."

At Crosstown Concourse, as the development is now called, the eight anchor organizations work together to leverage a cohesive understanding of health to fill lives with hope and joy. People of faith are not off to one side doing their own thing but are engaged with the community in a way that brings opportunity and change that people in the neighborhood have not seen in a long time. Health, arts, education, recreation, and small businesses come together to present a picture not only of individual wellness but of community wellness.

This is what makes Crosstown the logical embodiment of whole-person health that the Church Health Center is built upon. How do you bring rich and poor, white and black together? This is not the future just of the Church Health Center in Memphis but the future of the faith and health movement in America.

Here's a story from Scott that beautifully illustrates what it means to do life together in community.

One morning I saw an elderly woman who had been coming to us for a long time. At seventy-three, she was in good health, but on this day she seemed a little sad. I learned that her husband of fifty years had died three weeks earlier, after having prostate cancer for several years. She did everything for him, caring for him day in and day out. When he died, at first she felt a sense of relief—both for him and for herself. Now the boredom had set in. The funeral was over, people were not calling so frequently, and she felt alone.

She said, "Everything is over, but everything is not over."

I was able to offer her the opportunity to talk with our counselor, which she eagerly accepted. Then she remarked that she had always liked the Church Health Center and said, "This place is just so human."

I couldn't agree with her more. This place *is* so human. We are so human when we show compassion for people whose lives are in turmoil and who have seldom been treated with anything but disdain. But we are also so human when we fail to love and care for each other. We are so human when we have little surprises for children and fuel meaningful volunteer jobs for older people who feel used up, but we are so human because we overeat and underexercise.

Sharing our humanity means sharing both what we do right and what we do wrong. But when we get something wrong, we also get a chance to set it right.

Crosstown Concourse is giving the Church Health Center and all of Memphis a chance to do just that. It sets an incredible example of what's possible in cities and towns across the country.

Getting into Crosstown was a challenge. There's no question about it. The Church Health Center had to raise its share of funds for renovating the old Sears structure. And because the expanded space would allow them to serve more people and serve them better, their annual budget will have to be 50 percent higher going forward. But the Church Health Center is ready for the challenge. The slogan they adopted for the process of transitioning to Crosstown is "We were built for this."

Hear the conviction in that!

It does not imply there will be no uncertainty, no stumbling. It doesn't claim perfection. But it does convey that the organization understands its history enough to move forward in a way that will allow it to expand the depth and breadth of its services, both in Memphis and beyond. Working in partnership with like-minded groups and individuals will make them that much more effective at living a whole-person model of care. The environment of health care is changing, but the Church Health Center is building its capacity to thrive in the midst of change. And faith and health will always connect in the work of the Church Health Center.

And that's exciting!

Then Give Me Your Hand

"If your heart is like my heart, then give me your hand."

When Scott says this—as he often does—he is quoting John Wesley, who wrote on this subject in a sermon he called "Catholic Spirit" about maintaining affection even when beliefs may differ.

"Though we cannot think alike, may we not love alike?" Wesley said. "May we not be of one heart, though we are not of one opinion? Without all doubt, we may."

And later, "I do not mean, 'Be of my opinion.' You need not. I do not expect or desire it. I mean love me not in word only, but in deed and in truth."

This has been the spirit of the Church Health Center all along. And now it is the spirit of Crosstown Concourse.

Bound up in our shared humanity is our shared pilgrimage of health and faith. We journey together toward the heart of God.

The Bible is full of events that called together the people of God. Annual festivals, for example, were community events that included the poor, the widows and orphans, even the foreigners in Israel. A spirit of thanksgiving and worship marked the feasts. Was there food? Certainly. Was the food the main reason to gather? Certainly not.

Scott says, "At feast times in the Bible, the people of God were pilgrims who journeyed toward a sacred experience, an encounter with holiness. They journeyed toward stronger identity of what it meant to be God's community. They journeyed toward the abundance of God. Let me suggest instead that the core of the word *feast* relates to abundance not only of food but other healthy elements of our human pilgrimage—loved ones, laughter, connections, joy, hugs, faith. A feast gathers together varied elements into a shared festival of delight, no matter what the size of the group."

If your heart is like my heart, then give me your hand.

Finding a way to work together is more a matter of heart than head.

Crosstown will be a living, breathing experience of journeying toward the heart of God and the abundance we find there.

COMMUNITY CARES

I tend to work around four principles that give shape to my life, and I think they apply to how we learn to be good neighbors, hear each other's stories, learn from one another, and become companions on the journey toward a whole, well society, to touch the heart and soul of the humanity we share.

First, if you break it, you already own it. We've all seen the "If you break it, you buy it" signs in stores with fragile wares. Faith communities want people to come in our doors and join us, but we don't always take enough time to think about how our actions and presence affect a community. We should be careful that everything we do helps to build up the community the people we serve live in. Live lovingly. Live graciously. Life is fragile even at the community level. If we harm the community experience, or its experience of us as faith communities, then it's our responsibility to work toward restoration and rebuilding.

Second, as my grandfather used to often say, "Walk like me." Perhaps you've heard the story of the dog that did not have use of her hind legs. She gave birth to puppies with healthy legs, but because they watched their mama, they almost learned to move without using their back legs. Faith communities forget how powerful their examples can be. When a community does not seem to be going in a healthy direction, we must do more than lecture about what is wrong. The lecture is not helpful at all. Modeling a better way to go is far more likely to have a long-lasting influence.

Third, people need a place to belong. Though humans have been nomadic during points of history, I think this was an anomaly. The Creation story in the Bible talks about our having been created in a particular place. Human beings need a place that anchors us in times of windy seas. What better way to anchor a community than for congregations to live faithfully according to the values we consider so important? If we do this right, as we've talked about in this book, we will establish anchor points for individuals and families and communities to help them hold on to things that matter so they can flourish and grow toward wholeness, rather than be torn apart by flash points of the surrounding culture.

And finally, we are more than the sum of what we survive. If you've ever put together a secondhand jigsaw puzzle, you know the risk that edges will be torn or whole pieces will be missing, and the end result falls short of what you hoped it would be. People can feel that way about their lives. Too many broken pieces. Too many missing pieces. Too many pieces that don't quite fit together the way they should. And they look at their lives and think, *That's all I'm worth.* But every faith community, regardless of the religion it espouses, offers an interpretation of how life can be better and mean more because God loves us. Our value transcends our actions. It outshines our mistakes. It even surpasses our accomplishments. None of that defines what we are worth. God tells us what we are worth.

When I think about what I want my three daughters to understand as they go out into the world, I come back to these four truths. And the wholeness and health that I want for them is the same wholeness and health that my heart yearns to see on display in the society they will live in during the years to come. I hope that they—and you—will be eager to respond to the invitation to do God's work so that you, the ones you love, and the ones you serve will revel in an abundant life that comes from the heart of God.

Our God, we hunger and thirst in ways we do not fully understand. When our stomachs growl, we eat bread and it stops. But within our souls we have a deep hunger and we do not ever fully know how to make the pangs go away. Forgive us when we look to satisfy our hungers in ways that do not satisfy—in wealth, in wine, in all the false gods we surround ourselves with. Today let us eat the bread of life and be satisfied. Amen.